LET
FREEDOM
RING

LET
FREEDOM
RING

THOUGHTS ON THE
POLITICAL BETRAYAL OF AMERICA
AND THE
PEOPLES' COMING APOCALYPSE

M.G. MONTPELIER

CITI OF
BOOKS

CITIOFBOOKS, INC.
3736 Eubank NE Suite A1
Albuquerque, NM 87111-3579
www.citiofbooks.com
Hotline:1 (877) 389-2759
Fax:1 (505) 930-7244

Ordering Information:
Quantity sales. Special discounts are available on quantity purchases by corporations, associations, and others. For details, contact the publisher at the address above.

Printed in the United States of America.

ISBN-13:	Softcover	979-8-90124-304-6
	eBook	979-8-90124-305-3

FOR

A SUFFERING PEOPLE

OF

LIBERTY

POLITICALLY DECEIVED

ABANDONED AND FORGOTTEN

I am indebted to so many who have pursued the truth of freedom betrayed, especially Charles Derber, Thom Hartmann, Chris Hedges, Nancy MacLean, Hedrick Smith, Stuart Stevens, Richard Wolff, and Phil Robertson, for "proclaiming the truth of God's love" to an America ... "In God We Trust." A special note of gratitude to Professor Charles Derber for so many invaluable insights into the "surplus unworthy" of the Republican *"survival of the fittest"* America, and for so kindly allowing me to use language for the "Ruling High Table" from his book with Yale Magrass, *The Surplus American.* The political thoughts, comments, and opinions expressed in this work are mine unless otherwise noted.

FOR

DEMOCRACY

TO

LET FREEDOM RING

EVERY VOTE MATTERS

TABLE OF CONTENTS

DEDICATION i

ACKNOWLEDGEMENTS iii

UNITED STATES CONSTITUTION...................................... ix

POEM — GREED TRIUMPHANT.. 1
AUTHOR'S PREFACE... 3

POEM — LEFT TO DIE 10
ON FREE ENTERPRISE 12

POEM — LEST WE FORGET 16
THE HIGH TABLE 17

POEM — VOICE OF DESPAIR 22
A PEOPLE BETRAYED 23

POEM — TYRANNY OF GREED 42
CONSPIRACY OF EVIL 44

POEM — LIBERTY IN FLAMES 58
DEMOCRACY ON FIRE 59

POEM SENSELESS MISERY 76
HISTORICAL TRUTHS 77

POEM — FREEDOM 84
A PLANET IN CRISIS 85

POEM — A WORLD DEFILED 91
FOREVER WAR 92

POEM — PEACE SAY WE 100
DESPERATE LIVES 101

POEM — QUIET DESPERATION 115
BEYOND DARKNESS 116

POEM — FREEDOM LOST 131
FREEDOM OR FASCISM 132

POEM — AWAKE AMERICA 142
THE 1984 REALITY 143

POEM — FREEDOM CALLING 152
ON AMERICAN DEMOCRACY 153

POEM — EVERY VOTE MATTERS 158
TRUTH MATTERS 159

POEM — TO BEGIN ANEW 174
PROJECT 2025 176

POEM — FREEDOM RISING 183

UNITED STATES CONSTITUTION

Preamble: We the People of the United States, in Order to form a more perfect Union, establish Justice, insure domestic Tranquility, provide for the common defense, promote the general Welfare, and secure the Blessings of Liberty to ourselves and our Posterity, do ordain and establish this Constitution for the United States of America.

XIV Amendment: Section1. All persons born or naturalized ... are citizens of the United States and the State wherein they reside. No State shall make or enforce any law which shall abridge the privileges or immunities of citizens of the United States.

XIV Amendment: Section 3. No person shall be a Senator or Representative ... or hold any office ... having previously taken an oath...to support the Constitution of the United States ... [who] shall have been engaged in insurrection or rebellion against same, or given aid or comfort to the enemies thereof.

XV Amendment: Section 1. The right of citizens of the United States to vote shall not be denied or abridged by the United States or by any State on account of race, color or previous condition of servitude.

POEM

GREED TRIUMPHANT

TODAY AMERICA
"We the People"
are
A PEOPLE DECEIVED
by
REPUBLICAN GREED
and the
SUPREMACY OF WEALTH

TODAY AMERICA
"We the People"
are
A PEOPLE SUFFERING
from
MONOPOLY ECONOMICS
and the
DEREGULATION OF TRUTH

1

TODAY AMERICA
"We the People"
are
POLITICAL VICTIMS
of
"PROJECT 2025"
and the
POWER OF CORRUPTION

PREFACE

LET FREEDOM RING is a compendium of essays and poems from my published works on the Conservative Fifty-Year Republican "Assault on America," from the 1971 "Powell" strategic "grand design" to *"save capitalism from democracy"* and the 1981 Republican "Trickle Down" Revolution to the 2024 Republican power grab for restructuring American democracy into a "fascist" authoritarian America. The narrative is a reflective commentary coupled with facts from the historical record on the political-economic reality of America's dysfunctional "dark money" politics in today's Conservative Orwellian world of lies, deception and deceit.

My views center on today's reality that we are a People of Liberty politically and economically abandoned as *"just surplus"* struggling to survive in a Republican wasteland of concentrated wealth, ideological extremism, hypocrisy and betrayal.

To every working American struggling to make ends meet, **Let Freedom Ring** is both an

> **APPEAL** for political redress in the battle to overcome the Conservative *"survival of the fittest"* politics of today's

Republican world of "Trickle-Down" human bondage, and a

PLEA for a Citizen Electoral Mandate to end the Republican political-economic predatory culture of injustice, poverty, and death.

For me and the generation of 1945 to 1975, we were once a middle class people prosperous and secure. That was before the 1971 Republican "grand design" to *save capitalism from democracy"* and the making of the Conservative financialized predatory debt-based economy. Then, every American shared in some way the good times of America's Industrial Golden Age. We were a hard working industrious people, stable and strong, with a progressive living wage, an affordable mortgage, medical care, education, and the promise of a dignified retirement in old age.

Not to be forgotten, it was also the grand moment of the American experience, as we, a People of Liberty, pledged unequivocally our sacred honor to defend the "Constitution of the United States" against all enemies "foreign and domestic," and "national interest" meant, in real tangible terms, safeguarding the "general Welfare" of a free democratic people. After five decades of the Republican "Pooring of America," that once middle class affluence is now a Social Darwin subsistence-wage debt-based casino America of concentrated power and wealth.

America in every sector of American life is a Republican political-economic autocracy of monopoly supremacy, subsistence-wages, financial growth gimmicks, speculation schemes, and the destructive hedge fund pillaging of America's infrastructure. And so, we are a people consigned to endure today's Republican *"surplus left behind"* America of *"every man for himself"* struggling to secure the basic necessities of life.

With the onset of the 1971 Powell "grand design" to *"save capitalism from democracy,"* the rise and impact of the Business Round Table, Heritage Foundation, Cato Institute, and Federalist Society, coupled with a politicized Conservative Supreme Court's decisions granting unlimited, unaccountable "dark money" campaign funding, the integrity of America's democratic institutions have gradually become undermined, compromised, and lost in what is today's "Project 2025" plan to dismantle America's democratic institutions.

The historical perspective today suggests that the deaths of President Kennedy in 1963 and Martin Luther King, Jr. in 1968, were not only to be the demise of an envisioned "new frontier" and the beginning of a new era of "equality" in America, but the opening round of "dark money" white power conspiracies in the coming political-economic transformation of democracy to autocracy in America.

The ruthless, fanatical Republican decade's assault on America's People of Liberty today is the Social Darwin Political Economy of Conservative "dark money" vested interest Republican *"every man for himself"* political agenda. Whether or not we are willing to admit the truth to ourselves, we are a struggling democratic people mercilessly abandoned to the greed, corruption, and injustice of the Conservative predatory subsistence debt-based casino economy.

We are a people in a life struggle not only for the welfare of our families and our children's future, but what's to come of a disenfranchised hijacked America. In these desperate and perilous times we bear witness to the plight of millions of suffering Americans sacrificed and abandoned as just *"surplus unworthies"* to the ravages of the Social Darwin Conservatism of "you're on your own" desperation of want and despair. Hear we must, the lament of Charles Bukowski: ***"What a weary time to have the desire and the need to live but not the ability."***

The time is now we keep in mind as a People of Liberty the warning of Daniel Webster to America: ***"Our destruction should it come ... will be from the inattention of the people to the concerns of their government ... falling prey to the dupes of designing men and become the instruments of their own undoing."***

We are in this American moment a politically polarized nation given to Republican lies, false narratives, legislative chaos, extreme gun violence, and *"white supremacy"* politics. Considering the political extremism of the Republican controlled "House" of political extremists, the unlimited campaign "dark money" of the financial power elite, Republican voter district gerrymandering and voter suppression laws, we can expect the 2026 election will be exposed to every Conservative political resource of political extremism.

For a reminder of what a Republican power grab in 2026 will bring to America, imagine for a moment the tyranny and horror of Republican authoritarian rule over a "lawless" racist America of anger, hate, and chaos, unfettered predatory capitalism, and the terror of unbridled forever gun violence on the streets of America. The Republican Machiavellian "Project 2025" agenda is the promised Orwellian political supremacy master plan for a Conservative America of absolute power, concentrated wealth, and political retribution against the "enemy within," enemies of Constitutional democratic values committed to an America of Liberty, Justice, and the Rule of Law.

See we must the political reality before us of today's Republican "Project 2025" political offensive to restructure America's democratic institutions into a corrupt "fascist" autocracy. To date we have seen no less than:

(1) "day one" dictatorship;

(2) elimination of America's USAID international relief assistance program;

(3) dismantling of America's democratic order, institutions, and infrastructure;

(4) rollback of basic "civil rights: suppression of free speech, political assault on the media, law firms, science, the judiciary, and universities;

(5) mass firing of career non-political "civil servants" and removal of key government executives with political loyalists,

(6) aggressive enactment of the Republican "white supremacy" racist agenda;

(7) import tariffs levied on goods entering the US, paid by the consumer, spiking the cost of almost everything increasing the cost of living, and food prices now beyond the ability of some half of the population to meet basic needs;

(8) Republican 'big "terrible" bill' legislation giving the

Ultra-Rich trillion dollar tax cuts [and Argentina $40 billion], while cutting billions from affordable healthcare and food assistance spiking the cost of healthcare and medical insurance, and forced hospital closings across America;

(9)   state "prosecution" of political enemies;

(10) deployment of federal troops to "democratic" cities to contain and attack the "enemy within";

(11) people seized from the streets of America without warrant or due process by masked government agents many never to be seen again;

(12) use of "tear gas" and "assault weapons" against the Civil population in urban city neighborhoods by masked armed militia; and

There it is! The Republican Conservative "Project 2025" reality of today's Republican America: a 1930s racist authoritarian model of state "fascism."

Is this to be America's *"forever reality"* in a Republican authoritarian political world of tomorrow? America's political future now depends on us, People of Liberty willing to **EMBRACE** an America *"In God We Trust"* and **RESTORE** America to a democracy of secure democratic institutions, a strong middle class, and a prosperous America of *"Liberty and Justice for All."*

Without question the Conservative extremist establishment in 2026 will make every effort to "burn or rule" in a grand finale

"Assault on Democracy" to maintain absolute political power in both houses of the Congress. This is America's one time electoral moment where the future of America's Constitutional "checks and balances" for a Democracy of Freedom and Justice is up for grabs. Any one ballot cast in 2026 could be the deciding ballot that ultimately "PRESERVES OR DESTROYS" the future of democracy in America.

My hope is **LET FREEDOM RING** will be a wake up call for real grass roots democracy in 2026. The outcome of this struggle is nothing less than Freedom itself. Freedom for a people of Democracy, Truth, and Justice liberated from the Republican Corruption and Injustice of today's *"Profit over People" "survival of the fittest"* America of want, desperation, and despair.

M.G. Montpelier

FOR
DEMOCRACY
TO
LET FREEDOM RING
EVERY VOTE MATTERS

POEM

LEFT TO DIE

Across America
A Surplus People
"Left to Die"
Struggle to survive
Conservative "Trickle-Down"
Greed and Corruption

Across America
A Surplus People
Subsist
On Conservative"
"Trickle-Down"
Want and Desperation

Across America
A Surplus People
Struggle between
Darkness and Oblivion
Conservative Laissez-Faire
"Trickle-Down" Madness

Across America
A Surplus People
Hope each new day
For Freedom's Return
To an America of
Liberty and Justice for All

ON FREE ENTERPRISE

With
President
FRANKLIN ROOSEVELT

"True individual freedom cannot exist without economic security and independence ... Freedom means the supremacy of human rights everywhere. Our support goes to those who struggle to gain those rights and keep them. Our strength is our unity of purpose."

"Unhappy events abroad have taught us two simple truths about the liberty of a democratic people. The FIRST TRUTH is that the liberty of a democracy is not safe if the people tolerate the growth of private power to a point where it becomes stronger than the democratic itself. That, in its essence, is Fascism – ownership of Government by an individual, by a group, or by any other controlling private power. The SECOND TRUTH is that the liberty of a democracy is not safe if its business system does not provide

employment and produce and distribute goods in such a way as to sustain an accepted standard of living."

"Among us today a concentration of private power without equal in history is growing. This concentration is seriously impairing the economic effectiveness of private enterprise as a way of providing employment for labor and capital and as a way of assuring a more equitable distribution of income and earnings among the people of the nation as a whole ... Of all the corporations reporting, less than 5 per cent of them owned 87 per cent of all the assets of all of them ... less than 4 per cent of them earned 84 per cent of all the net profits of all of them. In 1929 [before the crash] three-tenths of 1 per cent of our population received 78 per cent of the dividends..."

"We believe in a way of living in which political democracy and free enterprise for profit should serve to protect each other – to ensure a maximum of human liberty not for a few but for all ... Today's answer on the part of the average man and woman ... is that if there is a danger it comes from that concentrated private economic power which is struggling so hard to master our democratic government."

"Private enterprise is ceasing to be free enterprise and is becoming a cluster of private collectivisms: masking as a system of free enterprise after the American model ... in fact becoming a concealed cartel system ... We all want efficient industrial growth and the advantages of mass production [that] has evolved into banker control of industry. We oppose that. Interlocking financial controls have taken from American business much of its traditional

virility, independence, adaptability and daring – without compensating advantages. They have not given the stability they promised." "One of the primary causes of our present difficulties, in the disappearance of price competition in many industrial fields ... When prices are privately managed at levels above those which would be determined by free competition, everybody pays ... price controls interfere with the ability of free enterprise to fill the needs of the community and provide employment for capital and labor ... If free enterprise is left to its own devices ... as it is today, it obviously cannot adjust itself to meet the needs and the demands of the country ... monopolistic controls which each business group imposes for its own benefit, inevitability destroys the buying power of the nations as a whole."

"It is of course necessary to operate the competitive system of free enterprise intelligently ... Examination of methods of conducting and controlling private enterprise which keep it from furnishing jobs or income or opportunity ... is long overdue ... No people, least of all a democratic people, will be content to go to work or to accept some standard of living which obviously and woefully falls short of their capacity to produce. No people, least of all a people with our traditions of personal liberty, will endure the slow erosion of opportunity for the common man, the oppressive sense of helplessness under the domination of a few, which are overshadowing our whole economic life."

"The power of a few to manage the economic life of the nation must be diffused among the many or be transferred to the public and its democratically responsible government.

If prices are to be managed and administered, if the nation's business is to be allotted by plan and not by competition, that power should not be vested in any private group or cartel … We must find practical controls over blind economic forces as well as overly blindly selfish men. Government can deal and should deal with blindly selfish men … I recommend that Congress [enact legislation to] effectively control the operation of bank holding companies [and] that this legislation make provision for the gradual separation of banks from holding company control or ownership … Business monopoly in America paralyses the system of free enterprise … and is fatal to those who manipulate it."

President
Franklin Roosevelt
Message to Congress
April 29, 1938

FOR
DEMOCRACY
TO
LET FREEDOM RING
EVERY VOTE MATTERS

POEM

LEST WE FORGET

Remember we must
They came promising
"Trickle-Down" Prosperity
Then
Repealed the rule of law
Took our jobs and pensions
Undermined our civil liberties
And
Freedom was no more
Greed enveloped the land
Corruption reigned supreme
As
Fascism Triumphed in
The Suffering Silence
Of Human Bondage

THE HIGH TABLE

"It really comes down to basic economics.
There's no comparative advantage for business in
America anymore. The only legitimate goal of our
companies is to make money ... We can only do that by
investing where labor is cheap ... taxes are nonexistent
and governments are too weak to stop us ... We are
simply doing what good capitalists ... have always done."
Derber and Magrass
The Surplus American

HIGH TABLE
ANNIVERSARY CONFERENCE
OPENING REMARKS

Chairman: "Ladies and gentlemen. Welcome to our 50th anniversary conference to discuss our national management of the nation's surplus population and this years' critical ongoing events that require our immediate attention.

As you all know, in the 1970s ... *the United States went into economic decline, after the costs of the Vietnam War and the rise of Europe and Japan ... Clearly, a major source of the trouble in America was that workers, especially educated and unionized workers infected by the 1960s revolts, felt too entitled. They were trying to interfere with our prerogative to run our corporations and to run the world. There was excessive democracy, a democratic distemper that had to be contained."*

"We got the American people to agree we had to spend more on armaments as they accept a declining standard of living, while big business profits soar. They identified with us, and our interests became their interest. They ... see themselves as part of a great American nation."

And so the Republican "Trickle-Down" 1981 *"Revolution opened the world to us by crushing the unions and creating trade agreement[s] ... that ensure us global profits. The government subsidized our shift to production abroad ... and won the support of the lower classes by making America the Great Superpower again and telling them that money given to us will Trickle-Down to the [the people ... but will provide] more money for us billionaires, lower taxes, fewer regulations ... with no conditions."*

Actually, the hard truth is that maintaining factories in America had become too expensive. We used the Trickle-Down free trade and tax policies as incentive to close the remaining American steel mills and America's industrial infrastructure and move production where labor is cheap, where we don't have to worry about environment or occupational health and safe standards.

Of course, *in America, with factories closing, inner cities are being abandoned. The jobs that gave blue-collar access to a middle class lifestyle ... disappeared. The American dream became an illusion. Rather than wealth trickling down, the gap between rich and non-rich has grown dramatically. This, my friends, is the legacy of the Republican Trickle-Down Revolution. Our Conservative legacy is more prosperity for more billionaires. Surely, the streets of the Trickle-Down revolution are lined with gold."*

That said, *"we must address today the fact that we have special problems to consider this year, as the number of "parasites and unworthy surplus rabble is increasing rapidly ... with ten million new unemployed in the last year. This, of course, is consistent with our business strategies over the last four decades ... and it demonstrates how profitable our national outsourcing ... has been."*

"We are seeing ... today the more we can outsource our financial services and dispose of surplus workers, the more profitable our operations have become. The problem is the unworthy elements of the surplus people, the parasite and freeloaders, are questioning the virtues of our national downsizing and outsourcing strategy. I know you all appreciate that surplus people are responsible for their own fate. Life is a privilege and they haven't earned it. They naturally blame the system rather than themselves for their unemployment and uselessness. Nevertheless, we've known from the beginning that while the surplus population we created would get Americans to do just about anything ... at minimum wages, in time it would have down the road ramifications. And that time is now before us."

"I realize that many don't want to hear that consumer debt is rising along with government debt. But this is very dangerous not just for the US but for the world economy. Deficits are not a problem as long as they stimulate productivity. The Trickle-Down "supply side" policies of the 1980s created massive deficits with huge government spending on the military and huge subsidies for big business that provided a short-term boom for billionaires. Our policies, however, have undermined our long-term competitive advantage by demonizing government, unraveling our industrial infrastructure, and romanticizing the military ... The protesters in the street know this."

We must now take advantage of the Republican political triumph of 2024. This is a one time opportunity to fulfill our decades goal for a Social Darwin "political economy." The Republican Congress, with encouragement from the Conservative Supreme Court, and with our political support, must move quickly to enact our long-awaited Conservative "Project 2025" agenda for *"surplus people [taking responsibility] for their own fate."* NO more Social Security, Medicare, and Medicaid; NO more welfare and food assistance programs for the "parasites" and "freeloaders;" NO more "socialist" programs that contribute to the national debt. And finally, NO more government intervention in the economy or the lives of the street people.

"There it is ladies and gentlemen. I appreciate your being here despite today's protests by the surplus people ... This is the biggest domestic disorder so far. We anticipated these protests, but not on a national scale ... We know our "surplus policy" marginalizes the masses and doesn't offer them even the illusion that they have any place in our society. I'm sure most of you agree it is in our best interest that this must change, and fast ... The surplus masses have

nothing to lose. It is imperative all of us here support the massive shift in our political strategy *for the reconstruction of our own country.* (pause)

Now, if we don't wrap up the meeting today, we'll convene again tomorrow until all presentations have been heard. Please enjoy the rest of your evening.

**FOR
DEMOCRACY
TO
LET FREEDOM RING
EVERY VOTE MATTERS**

POEM

VOICE OF DESPAIR

Suspended in a sea of Corruption,
Poverty, and Despair, I ask myself
"Who Am I" in this Political
Wasteland of Lies and Deceit

Across the Landscape of Freedom,
I see the face of Darkness and Pain
Of Suffering People longing for
Liberty, Truth, and Justice

And in my trepidation, I know
I am nothing, just "Trickle-Down"
Fodder struggling in a Lives for
Profit Predatory Jungle

With each new day I strive to
Survive the Deprivation of
Being "surplus" in a wilderness of
Greed, Corruption, and Injustice

Betrayed, Abandoned, Forgotten
To subsist in Economic Human
Bondage, I live for the return of
Democracy, Freedom, and Truth

A PEOPLE BETRAYED

*"Your purpose, then, plainly stated, is
that you will destroy the Government,
unless you be allowed to construe and
enforce the Constitution as you please.
You will rule or ruin in all events."*
Abraham Lincoln
Cooper Union Address, 1860

SUNDAY MORNING

A beautiful morning. The sun is shining; not a cloud in
the sky; a soft breeze in the air. A great morning just to be
alive. Bill and Martha have just returned home from Sunday
church service.

As Bill relaxes quietly in his chair, Martha happily goes
about preparing their usual Sunday brunch. Martha looks
over at Bill, smiles, and says, "Bill, you look as if you have
the weight of the world on your shoulders." Bill opens his
eyes and smiles at Martha. "Just thinking, my Dear. Did you
notice the church was over half empty this morning?"

"That's every Sunday, Bill," Martha replies. "I suspect people have come to believe that faith doesn't matter. It's as if God doesn't have a place in their lives anymore."

"It's more than that," Martha," Bill responds. "At its core it's everything that personifies the Conservative *"every man for himself"* ideological culture of death. Do you realize it's now fifty years since the financial gurus hijacked the Republican party and set about dismantling America's manufacturing prosperity and restructuring America for the sole benefit of the financial power elite? January's Capitol Insurrection to overturn the Constitution is just the culminating event of decades of radical Republican ideological extremism to usurp the people's sovereignty in a final bid for absolute power and the concentration of wealth.

"The Republican Conservative struggle for the Soul of America has been long and unrelenting. What's left, I'm afraid, is the everyday reality that most Americans today struggle to just make it another day. Everything's temporary, Martha, with no thought of the future. I have no doubt that in the fullness of time the "truth" will reveal the extent of the Republican Conservative legislative demise of the American Dream, the middle class, the death of competitive free market capitalism, and the making of America's debt-based financial economy of minimum-wage jobs. And the Conservative reality of "nothingness" is ever present in every sphere of America life.

"Today, Martha, concentrated wealth and the Pooring of America are the dominant political-economic features of a decadent America. I often wonder how many of today's voters understand that the 1% own more than the entire middle class, while three billionaires own more than the bottom 50% of America.

"It seems not so long ago, Bill, prosperity shone brightly over an America pleased with itself, healthy and alive," says Martha. "You're getting old, Martha," replies Bill with a chuckle. "But you're right."

"There was a time not so long ago when the people of America were at economic peace, stable and secure with a strong industrial middle class where everyone had access to a secure productive living-wage job, affordable healthcare, education and housing, and the promise of retirement with dignity in old age.

"All that once seemed to be for a prosperous middle class is now gone, Martha. All that promise of yesterday's America is no more. All that was democracy in America that gave life meaning and happiness has been dismantled and discarded to the greed of fairy-tale profits and a financialized debt-based casino economy at the expense of an abandoned "surplus" people *responsible for their own fate.*"

"And sadly for our children and grandchildren, Bill, all we once cherished that was an America founded on the Sovereignty of the People, the Blessings of Liberty, and the protection of the "general Welfare" is now all but yesterday's promise lost to an impoverished predatory America of individual extremism, greed and corruption."

"This has all come about because we've lost as a people so much of our understanding of truth and freedom. We've suppressed our traditional principles and democratic values in this new "age of political disinformation." Everything is a socially constructed falsehood to achieve a needed political end, and the greatest of lies is taken for truth. The ugliness of denial that we've come to accept has allowed for total revolution through deceit, identity politics, and social engineering to where we see before us the reality of a Conservative draconian world of the "survival of the fittest" where the elderly, the disabled, the poor and the homeless are at risk."

"But, in a sense, it's more that, Bill. With our acceptance of the denial of truth, we've lost our sense of the sacred, empathy for our neighbor's plight, and what gives life meaning. We've lost our understanding of democratic freedoms for an America that's been sold a bill of goods. I believe if enough of us were to begin to buy in to the formative truth of God's love, we would see God's saving power take hold of this country. We'd see a country once again committed to the reality of truth; a country of virtuous leaders committed to an America of Liberty and Justice for all; laws that stand up for everyone's 'inalienable right to life'; a return to civility and the brotherly love that transcends greed, division, and hate."

II

Everyone's talking. But no
One speaks truth to the how
We are a suffering people
Subsisting in human bondage

No one talks of the Republican
Conservative politics of radical
Extremism, absolute power,
And the *"survival of the fittest"*

No one speaks to the tyranny of
The Republican political fanaticism
*"To virtually eliminate the middle
Class"* of a free democratic people

No one talks of the Republican
Political carnage and desolation
Of today's America of Want,
Desperation, and Despair

No one bears witness to the
Fifty-Year betrayal and plunder of
America's *"Profit before People"*
Republican *"Trickle-Down"* politics

Now, after more than forty years of autocratic Republican legislative governance, the people of America are again asking in the quiet silence of their distress and despair that never ending question: **Why?**

> **WHY** is America a nation of excessive income inequality, hallowed-out bankrupt communities, decimated families, structural racism, political corruption, and divisive polarization?

> **WHY** is America unable to employ its people with secure living-wage jobs, provide a decent "standard of living,"

affordable healthcare, education, food, and housing, and a secure dignified retirement?

WHY is more than one out of two Americans living poor struggling to make ends meet in the richest country in the world?

WHY does America tolerate sacrificing *"Lives for Profit"* in a democracy founded on *"the inalienable right to life"*?

WHY in the *"Promised Land of Democracy, Truth, and Justice* do so many who take the "oath of office" to *"support, protect, and defend"* the people turn their back on the people? And,

"WHY," why are we an abandoned "surplus" people struggling to exist in an America of concentrated wealth and despair in the richest country in the world?

ISN'T IT TIME AMERICA WE UNDERSTAND WHO WE ARE AS A PEOPLE OF LIBERTY?

To comprehend the political, cultural, and economic realities of this American moment is to understand the "truth" lies buried, all but hidden from the *"inattention of the people to the concerns of their government,"* concealed by deception, lies, and false promises. America's presidents for decades have cautioned the nation to "face the truth."

The FOUNDING FATHERS *cautioned against the rise of concentrated economic power that takes away liberty;*

JIMMY CARTER in his 1979 presidential address, *"Crisis of Confidence," warned America that today's government "designed for the people" has "gotten into the hands ... of special interests ... an invisible empire ... set up above the forms of democracy;"*

ABRAHAM LINCOLN *warned of the greed and corruption of the "money powers;"*

And, the Republican President **THEODORE ROOSEVELT** *spoke of an "invisible government owing no allegiance ... that sits enthroned "behind the ostensible government."*

History's warning is today's American reality. In sharp contrast to America's Declaration of Independence and Constitutional guarantees enacted to protect the "general Welfare," **the Republican "big money" ideological agenda of the last five decades has achieved the political economy of** *"every man for himself" individual extremism: the "freedom from of obligations; freedom from responsibility; freedom to fend for oneself" and the freedom to starve."*

Today we all experience in one way or another the Republican subsistence debt-based America of poverty wages and a subsistence standard of living. The Republican freedom of "individual extremism" is today the people's political-economic reality of the Conservative political license to steal and destroy in the name of profit. The Republican "Pooring of America" fulfills *DANIEL WEBSTER'S warning – that "our overthrow ... should it come ... will be ... from the inattention of the people to the concerns of their government ... falling prey to the dupes of designing men and become the instruments of their own undoing".*

And come they did in the 1980s with a vengeance. They came with the ruthlessness of the "designing men" of 1873, 1893, 1907, and 1929. **And in the 1980s the economic power brokers hyped the Republican "Trickle-Down" Revolution, DISMANTLED America's industrial economy, TRANSFORMED the people's manufacturing industrial base into a deregulated rogue economy of casino capitalism, and LAID THE GROUND WORK ground work for the dismantling of America's democratic institutions.**

This is the reality of the power of America's financial plutocracy, an American oligarchic monolithic system of political-economic dominance over American democracy that is at the heart of America's concentration of wealth in the top 1%, the "Pooring of America," and a 2008 financial collapse. The continual rise of today's inflationary surge of rising prices irrespective of the needs of the people is simply that the "laissez-faire" redistribution of the people's limited resources demonstrates that the deregulated "free" market economic system of supply and demand is dead. Should doubt remain, forget we not, the Republican lies, disinformation, and deceit that seek autocratic power supremacy lingers in our midst, and with the advent of "PROJECT 2025" holds captive the reality of truth that perpetuates inequality and injustice in every aspect of American life.

III

**We've heard the empty
promises of "designing men"**

**We've borne the trauma of
want, desperation, and despair**

**We've endured the treachery of
disloyalty, betrayal, and sedition**

**We've traveled the road of lies
to the reality of dictatorship**

Enter **James BUCHANAN**, the 1960s political economic "intellectual of the embattled Jim Crow South" and pioneer of the Conservative decades' Republican assault on America's democracy. In time Buchanan's political theories would disempower the electoral majority and shift people power to America's kleptocratic ruling elite. Buchanan believed that the people must be prevented from using the public power of representative democracy if the "supremacy of capital" was to survive. He saw an American world dominated by the wealthiest and most powerful. His goal was a private governing class of the financial power elite freed from public accountability. Buchanan's strategy became a secretive political agenda to revise the political dynamics of democratic governance.

CATHERINE MACLAIN, in *Democracy in Chains: The Deep History of the Radical Right's Stealth Plan for America,* describes how the political strategy Buchanan and his collaborators "developed to disempower the political majority." ***The Buchanan* stealth strategy, backed by unlimited "dark money," called for a "stealth takeover of the Republican**

Party as its delivery mechanism," and a stealth agenda to "kill off" the unions, limit voting rights, privatize everything from public resources to Social Security and Medicare, reframe the tax laws to limit wealthy taxation and direct taxation to the little people, deregulate the rule of law, deny climate change, and transform the legal system into "a new jurisprudence … to make the protection and enhancement of corporate profits and private wealth the cornerstone of the legal system."

The Republican political establishment, politically backed by unlimited "dark money," **in 1980 implemented Buchanan's political-economic theory of capital supremacy and the Powell strategic stealth plan for the Conservative takeover of America.** The Republican plan designed to *"save capitalism from democracy,"* focused on placing legal restraints on public officials to prevent them "from using public power," *take down democracy with a cadre of "true believers" for whom compromise is a dirty word," purge the party of "old time" Republicans, and "force elected officials" in every red state do the party's bidding or "lose their seats." Today the Republican Party of "old" is no more.*

In 1971 the Republican party elite came armed with the "Powell Memorandum," the strategic blueprint written by Lewis Powell to the U.S. Chamber of Commerce to save the " free enterprise system" from Democracy." The plan outlined the method and means to undermine America's democratic institutions, restructure the American economy to unhampered capital supremacy, and financially vandalize an economically secure democratic people. **Then in 1980, the new "hijacked" Republican political establishment embarked on a political propaganda campaign of lies and deceit promising "Trickle-**

Down" prosperity for "everyone, including the poor," in a skillfully scripted crusade shrouded in political smoke and mirrors.

The Republican Conservative ideological triumph of 1980 established the Republican political establishment as the delivery mechanism for implementing the Conservative subjugation and political take over of America's democracy. They drove to deindustrialize the people's prosperous economic prosperity into a "financialized" political economy, and eliminate the "middle class" majority as part of the Conservative strategic blueprint to reconstruct America into a kleptocracy of wealth, power, and privilege. The American economic apocalypse of today is the political-economic reality of those "designing men" of 1970, who **as Richard Clarke reminds us, sought** *"to virtually eliminate the middle class majority in America."*

This is the political-economic reality of the Conservative "political economy" promulgated by **James BUCHANAN** to disempower America's electoral majority from using the public power of representative government; **Milton FREIDMAN**, champion of deregulated "laissez-faire" markets and maximization of shareholder value as the sole purpose and social responsibility of capitalism; **Robert BORK**, advocate of operational efficiencies over competition through mergers and acquisitions; and **Lewis POWELL**, author of the 1971 Conservative grand strategic blueprint to *"save capitalism from democracy" promising 'universal prosperity for all' that delivered the people of America an engineered financialized subsistence debt-based casino economy of want, desperation, and despair.*

The Republican political-economic reality, today controlled by Conservative anti-democratic extremists, is the Republican new political order of "designing men" tasked to suppress democracy through the manipulative control of state power, and overthrow the ability of representative government to protect the "general Welfare" and the human and civil rights of a Constitutional America.

After decades of "Trickle-Down" financial greed and political corruption, this may well be America's world of tomorrow should "We the People" allow a Republican "voter suppression" seizure of power succeed in 2026. The human tragedy of the Conservative extremism of the "*survival of the fittest*" is at the threshold of becoming a forever Republican political-economic reality of oppression holding America hostage in an impoverished web of tyrannical greed and corruption.

IV

"The Private sector Thrives Best with Minimal State involvement ..." GOVERNMENT'S ROLE in the Conservative "Trickle-Down" state is limited to: "CONTROL the surplus population;" ADVANCE state policies that "eliminate" government regulation and wealthy and corporate taxation; PROVIDE for "off-shore" job incentives, corporate subsidies' and trade policies that send jobs abroad;" and to SUPPORT government disinvestment of America's infrastructure by describing the infrastructure itself as socialism."
Derber & Magrass,
The Surplus American

As the "designing men" of wealth, power, and greed proceeded to pillage and plunder America, dismantle the institutions of Constitutional democracy, curb the rights of the people, and ravage America's prosperous communities, they have destroyed

America's ability to employ its people with secure living-wage employment.

The domestic financial "colonization" of America is the political and economic reality of the takeover, subjugation, and "Pooring of America." **The Republican political establishment, bearer of the sword of Social Darwin imperialism and the ideology of the *"survival of the fittest,"* ruthlessly descended on the people of America in 1981 in pursuit of absolute power and capital supremacy over American democracy.**

In one historic electoral moment based on promises of false prosperity and national greatness, the Republican "Trickle-Down" Revolution, in the absence of any public scrutiny, gave rise to a new ruling power elite. The Conservative ideological political agenda of radical extremism gave way to a "survival of the fittest" political mandate to disenfranchise the American people, deconstruct American democracy, and financialize America. And in less than a decade the Republican political establishment accomplished history's greatest mass exploitation of a free democratic people.

The Republican "Trickle Down" Revolution that would come to revolutionize America's political and economic way of life, impoverish the American people, and institutionalize the unhampered supremacy of capital is the story of the financial takeover of America. It is also a chronicle of political-economic greed, political corruption, lies and deceit, and the power of "dark money" documented by Donald Bartlett and James Steel in *The Betrayal of the American Dream;* William Greider, *Who Will Tell the People;* Jane Mayer, *Dark Money;* Hedrick Smith,

Who Stole the American Dream, and Thom Hartmann, *Screwed: The Undeclared War Against the Middle Class.*

Tragically for today's America, few among us were listening, and fewer Americans to this day understand little of today's crushing reality of the Republican Fifty-Year unraveling of American democracy to the supremacy of capital and Conservative political-economic dominance over America.

V

**When
No One FEELS
The PAIN,
Desperation and Despair
Of a SUFFERING people
Exploited and Discarded**

**When
No One HEARS
The Cry of the
OPPRESSED
For Equal Justice
Before The Law**

**The
FLAME OF LIBERTY
Beckons brightly for an
ABANDONED PEOPLE
Longing for a life of
Peace and Security**

Lewis Powell saw the success of organized labor and the cry for human and civil liberties as a middle class *"assault on the free enterprise system"* and the cause for the decline in America's industrial profitability. His subsequent political manifesto formulated the Conservative ideological political strategy for the Republican political establishment to politically subvert American democracy, undermine the democratic political process, and subjugate the people of America to the disenfranchisement of a new politically created predatory "Trickle-Down" subsistence economy of concentrated wealth.

The Powell strategic blueprint for Republican political domination and concentration of wealth in the hands of a few triggered the mobilization of America's "big money" vested interests to embark on a quiet - low-key - long-term - well-funded political campaign to secure the transformation of American governance to *"save capitalism from democracy."*

The Republican political betrayal of America for a social-economic transformation of America and political-economic dominance over American democracy set in motion the Republican Conservative Supremacy Agenda.

> **FIRST** they moved to **REVOKE** the "rule of law" and oversight accountability through the **DEREGULATION** of finance, business, politics; and then **PROCEEDED** with relentless and ruthless resolve to:
>
> **ABOLISH** wealthy and corporate taxation through Republican trillion dollar tax cuts, tax rate deductions, and tax exemptions;
>
> **BUILD** a Conservative "Trickle-Down" predatory *"every man for himself" "survival of the fittest"* political economy of concentrated wealth;

CREATE a "white supremacist" majority in pursuit of a white nationalist Conservative agenda of ideological extremism and political dominance;

DECONSTRUCT the machinery of government, infrastructure, and America's democratic institutions;

DISMANTLE America's community-centered political infrastructure and with it America's ability to employ an abandoned "surplus"people "left to their own fate";

DISCREDIT free press journalism to shield and defend the Republican political "Trickle-Down" core agenda of political lies, disinformation, false narratives, and conspiracy theories to politically disrupt, divide, and polarize the American people;

ELIMINATE Social Security, Medicare, Medicaid and the Social Safety Net;

LAY the foundation for a political takeover of American democracy.

LIMIT voter access to the ballot through district gerrymandering, voter suppression laws, and voter certification barriers;

OBSTRUCT democratic populist policies and legislation that support the "common good" and "general Welfare" of the people;

PRIVATIZE public services, public lands, and America's natural resources to private sector contractors of "big money" political financial support;

POLITICIZE the Congress and Judiciary to enshrine private wealth, protect the laissez-faire economy of "Profit over People," block congressional oversight accountability, water-down government regulation, and stifle political reform;

REMOLD America's political, judicial, and academic state of mind to the Conservative mindset of "Trickle-Down" individual extremism;

SECURE political "dark money" dominance over state legislatures.

Today we struggle as a People of Liberty in an America dominated by an entrenched Conservative ideological Social Darwinism that is the Republican supremacy of capital and a democracy of want, desperation, and despair. The Republican four decades of politically engineered pillage and plunder of the American people has destroyed America's industrial prosperity, cultural values, and the well-being and security of the American family. The Republican political victory of radical Conservative extremism in unguarded electoral moments, especially in 1980, 2016, and 2024, is tragically the Conservative political-economic reality of this American moment.

VI

**Our strength is in the things
we value. The time is now we
assert who we are: either we
are a People of Liberty, or
WE ARE NOTHING!**

Overnight the Republican political establishment of 1980, gave birth to a Conservative "Trickle-Down" *"you're on your own"* political platform that shamelessly asserted American capitalism didn't *"need America any more …Surplus people are responsible for their own fate."* America ceased to be a nation of freedoms fought and won in the blood of our Sons and Fathers, the "Freedom from Want, Freedom from Hunger, and Freedom from Fear." These are the freedoms upon which ***President Franklin Roosevelt declared "Liberty requires an opportunity to make a living which gives not only enough to live by, but something to live for"*** Today the *"Blessings of Liberty"* have all but become entombed in an American graveyard of "imperial" greed and corruption.

The tragic reality is the "designing men" of wealth and power in our time have ruthlessly destroyed America's competitive "free market economy" of supply and demand. The economics of national prosperity for the many has been transformed into a laissez-faire "Trickle-Down" subsistence debt-based casino economy of monopoly power supremacy. America's democracy of the people has been politically transformed in every sector of American life into a "deregulated" state of debt liability taxation for the little people, and unavoidable poverty engendered by the power of concentrated wealth.

Our national inattention to the concerns of our government has led to the functional undoing of every governing institution, including the Supreme Court and the legislative branch, where precedent parliamentary procedure established over the centuries have been "politically" corrupted and manipulated to the Conservative political agenda. Every Republican act and word spoken is couched in the deceit, deception, and lies of political interests that consider the people "economically illiterate, culturally backward, and demographically irrelevant."

We see at every level of the Republican political establishment, ruthless "designing men" of wealth and power that seek to undermine the people's democratic process and seize absolute authoritarian power. These are the "designing men" **Vice President Henry Wallace warned America to beware of, the money changers, the profiteers, and the usurpers** *"who claim to be super patriots … but would destroy every liberty guaranteed by the Constitution; demand free enterprise, but … are spokesmen for monopoly and vested interests; their final objective … to capture political power [to] keep the common man in eternal subjugation."*

The Conservative politics of political dominance, individual extremism, and economic subjugation "overshadows" all that America values. For a democratic republic "of the people" committed to "Liberty and Justice for all," today's Conservatism of of lies, voter suppression, and white supremacy politics is the "fascist" road to autocracy.

The America of 2026 beckons every citizen of democracy to take an affirmative stand to restore America to a nation of Freedom, Equality, and Justice.

FOR
DEMOCRACY
TO
LET FREEDOM RING
EVERY VOTE MATTERS

POEM

TYRANNY OF GREED

TODAY AMERICA
"We the People"
Are
A PEOPLE DECEIVED
By
REPUBLICAN GREED
DARK MONEY TYRANNY
And
CONCENTRATED WEALTH

TODAY AMERICA
"We the People"
Are
A DESPERATE PEOPLE
From
REPUBLICAN CORRUPTION
And
VULTURE CAPITALISM

TODAY AMERICA
"We the People"
Are

A PEOPLE SUFFERING
From
REPUBLICAN DEREGULATION
And
CAPITAL SUPREMACY

CONSPIRACY OF EVIL

"When you see that in order to produce,
you need to obtain permission from men
who produce nothing -

"When you see that money is flowing to
to those who deal, not in goods, but
in favors -

"When you see that men get richer by graft
and by pull than by work, and your laws
don't protect you, but protect them
against you -

"When you see corruption being rewarded
and honesty becoming self-sacrifice -
you may see society is doomed.

Ayn Rand
Atlas Shrugged, 1957

Come to terms we must with today's reality we are suffering people of an American "Conspiracy of Evil" to "save capitalism for democracy" and usurp the power of the people to secure absolute power dominance over America. The time for autocratic governance finally came to fruition in 2024, with the Republican assumption of absolute power to implement the Conservative "Project 2025 agenda to *keep the common man in perpetual subjugation.*"

H. W. Brands reminds us that *"The essence of democracy is equality [while] the essence of capitalism is inequality."* Fascism in turn is the power of financial capital. Fascist movements rise when a group begins to lose power and makes the decision to sacrifice democracy in order to maintain power. This was the political-economic situation in the 1970s when the United States went into economic decline. The financial power elite believed the educated and unionized workers of America were trying to interfere with the prerogative of America's corporations to run the world. Democracy had to be contained.

The 1971 Powell Memorandum, as we've seen, was the political-economic reaction to America's decline in corporate profitability. The Powell strategic plan laid the foundation for the Republican decades-long *"assault on democracy"* through a protracted political process of **DEREGULATING** the "Rule of Law" in business and finance; **CREATING** a Conservative Social Darwin *"survival of the fittest"* predatory "political economy" of concentrated wealth; and **LAYING** the foundation for an autocratic takeover of absolute power in America.

With the Republican political triumph in 1980, millionaires turned into billionaires, a prosperous working class became the working poor, and after 35 years of "Trickle-Down" promises most Americans now live pay-check to pay-check, and not a single bit of America's booming prosperity has trickled down to the working people of America. Actually, The Republican governance of the 1980s lowered the top income tax for the 1% from 70% to 28%; enacted for the first time a tax on Social Security; tripled the national debt from $738 billion to $2.1 trillion; and through the Conservative politics of scorched earth deregulation turned America's industrial prosperity into today's subsistence debt-based casino society of want, desperation, and despair. We became, as Jim Hightower relates in *Thieves in High Places*, *"a people ruled by thieves"* [controlled] *"by a ruling class of moneyed elites that usurps liberty transferring money and power from the many ... to the few."*

Welcome to the Conservative *"survival of the fittest"* predatory world of "surplus" people *"responsible for their own fate."* In today's Republican world of "Lives for Profit" radical individual extremism, the ideology of the "survival of the fittest" offers "freedom" without responsibility to a privileged power elite. For the rest of America, the Republican ideological imperative of "individual extremism" has become the "freedom" to fend for oneself, support a family on a subsistence-wage, the absence of affordable healthcare, and to survive in any meaningful way.

The Republican subsistence "Trickle-Down society promised "prosperity for everyone" in 1980 and destroyed America's capitalism of free competition, gutted America's industrial prosperity, and financialized the American economy into a political-economic engine of wealth concentration for the top 1%. And characteristic of the lies and deceit of greed and corruption of the Republican "Trickle-Down" miracle of wealth creation, there followed financial scandals of corporate fraud, insider trading, foreclosure abuse, stock manipulation, financial growth gimmicks, hedge fund profiteers, and the "soft money" plunder of America's worker pension funds. The "invisible hand" of fluctuating markets exploded in the 2008 financial collapse, and, the taxpayers provided the multi-trillion-dollar bailouts that continue to this day to add trillions to the national debt.

Between 1981 and 2000, America's productivity increased by some 70% while wages remained all but stagnant. And the earnings of the top 1% and 0.1% increased 158% and 341% respectively. For the "surplus" left behind *Time* (August 2/9, 2021) reports that since 1979 the cumulative change in real hourly wages for American workers rose but 3% for the bottom 10 percent and 15% for the middle third of the workforce. Tragically, the record also shows that the top 1% own America while over half of America's workers subsist on a low-wage income *"making an average wage of $10.22 an hour."*

Look around the neighborhood, open up the newspaper, turn on the evening news, and we see a people of democracy polarized and divided by the radicalized extremism of truth denied, racial xenophobia, political violence, and the inability of the average American to sustain the basic needs of life.

The people's economy is unrecognizable from a generation ago with an impoverished *"survival of the fittest"* America of at least 180 million Americans living poor or on the edge of poverty; two out of three working Americans existing on a subsistence-wage while over 50 million Americans, including 15 million children, go to bed hungry. We see a Republican politically engineered society of "surplus" people desperately trapped in a ruthless quagmire of institutional decay struggling in silent desperation for the sole benefit of the financial power elite.

Everywhere we look we see the suffering and pain and ever present carnage and desperation of the Fifty-Year Republican "Pooring of America," from the tens of thousands of rusting factories to the latest shut down of America's remaining automotive manufacturing plants. We feel the distress and misery of an abandoned "surplus" people politically condemned to the "Trickle-Down collateral damage of the Republican financialized *freedom to choose"* culture of death: a Conservative ideological universe of unrelenting political decadence. We see a democratic people politically ravaged economically and morally condemned to subsist in bankrupt impoverished communities all across America. We saw a free democratic people victimized from the annual trauma of over 100,000 "opioid" deaths, 90,000 suicides, 40,000 violent gun deaths, including some 1,000 massacres.

This is the everyday reality of the Republican "Trickle Down" America of the *"survival of the fittest."* The Republican ownership of death and suffering is the America of "anything goes" in the pursuit of Profit and Power at any cost: as with the unregulated Big Pharma's multi-billion dollar "opioid" profit scheme that killed over a million Americans, a burning planet fueled by fossil energy profits, and a Republican violent "insurrection" to overturn the will of the people.

II

"America's megabanks and policy makers are continuing a program the ultimate result of which is to virtually eliminate the middle class majority in America," Richard Clark writes in *"Why is America Suffering?"* Yesterday's American prosperity is today an America of consolidated wealth, the demise of wealthy and corporate taxation, capital supremacy, and for everybody else,

an America of "every man for himself" In 1981, Republican legislation reduced wealthy taxation from a 70% high to less than 10%, 7.2% for millionaires, and 3.2% for the top one tenth percent of America's taxpayers. 83% of the Republican trillion "tax cut" of 2017 went to the top 1% and reduced the corporate tax rate from 35% to 21%. In 2020, the wealth of the richest 1% of Americans increased by over $7 trillion while the 55 most profitable companies in America paid "zero" taxes, and the 400 wealthiest households paid an overall tax rate less than any income group in America. How is it in America any individual can hold a $500 million a year position and pay virtually no taxes? Well, it's not difficult to understand when we realize, as one of America's most privileged aristocratic elite famously remarked, *"Only the little people pay taxes!"*

America in 2023 had *"the widest wealth gap between the rich and the poor of any industrial country."* We see America's billionaires today worth more than double the cumulative wealth of the bottom 156 million poorest Americans. According to Professor Davis Markovits of the Yale Law School: *"the richest 5% of American households own two-thirds of the country's total wealth … The economic inequality that separates the rich from the rest of us has become so great … [that] to reduce inequality and honor shared citizenship is to tax wealth … World history teaches that oligarchies are almost impossible to unwind … Extreme wealth inequality confronts the U.S. with a civilizational threat. Wealth taxes answer the threat."*

The Conservative "core values" that drive the Republican "Culture of Death" in America hold in common the Social Darwin political-economic theory of the "survival of the fittest," the "superiority" of a ruling elite, and every human being is *"responsible for his own fate."* Everything on the planet is a commodity subject to the taking of the power brokers in pursuit of profit and wealth." *"Human beings,"* as Samuel Goldman points out, *"are raw material to be used or disposed of ... in a disenchanted world of slavery and terror."*

The Conservative extremism of "power dominance" and the "survival of the fittest" rationalized by the American political economists Buchanan, Friedman, and Bork to justify the "Pooring of America," is today the "dark money" America of political economy, wealth concentration, and monopoly dominance. We are as a "surplus" people just "collateral damage" persevering in a subsistence-wage universe, rising unaffordable cost of living; a national debt of some $367 trillion; over 150 billion dollars of medical debt; some 2 trillion dollars in "forever" student loan debt; and over 15 trillion dollars in credit card debt.

The sad reality for America today is as the French historian Georges Lefebvre laments in *The Coming of the French Revolution:* *"I look with compassion upon the cruel tempest with which my country is threatened, I shed tears to see so many ... reduced to such a profound misery."*

III

Since the dawn of the Republican "Trickle-Down" Revolution of 1980, four decades of Republican political dominance has reduced over half the population of America to a state of human desperation. This is the political-economic condition of America that came with the rise of unhampered capital supremacy, the Pooring of America, and the death of America's industrial economic lifeline. With the loss of secure living-wage jobs in every mill town across America, the security and stability of America's once prosperous middle class disappeared, and the people of America became just discarded "surplus" labor in a subsistence debt-based casino economy of all are *"responsible for their own fate."*

The heart of the Republican "Trickle-Down" Revolution was the deindustrialization of America's manufacturing economy and the outsourcing of American labor to off-shore cheap foreign labor and big profits. And thus we became a nation of privatized public services, the creation of a Republican legislated money-driven economy of financial instruments and debt-based poverty.

In the 1960s, before the rise of the Conservative Revolution of the *"survival of the fittest"* subsistence *"every man for himself"* economy, the United States produced 96% of what it consumed. Hundreds of thousands of mill towns and factory cities across America supported an economic miracle the envy of the world. America's children graduated from high school to work in local industries secure in a lifetime of stable family living-wage jobs, affordable family healthcare, and the promise of a dignified retirement. Downtown America prospered and life was good in an American world that offered a strong standard of living that provided an affordable family home, family vacation, and the promise of opportunity for the next generation.

With the elimination of America's manufacturing prosperity, hundreds of thousands of mill towns and factory cities across America lost their livelihood and reason for existence. Tens of millions of jobs lost forever, whole industries wiped out, and America's working class deprived of productive meaningful work.

All that remained were hollowed out towns of once prosperous small businesses, and the rise of monopoly owned box-stores, strip malls of fast-food franchises, and discount stores, and widespread poverty. America became a parking lot of bankrupt communities struggling to survive the shock, horror, and desperation of instant poverty with no available means of survival.

An abandoned factory town is not just a plant closing. It's a street scene from the apocalypse, the removal of all that gives life, meaning, and purpose to the community. Without work, the life-blood of the community evaporates. People are left isolated, helpless, and desperate; marriages and families fall apart while civil institutions and community church life die slowly. As the economic deprivation of the community intensifies, the social fabric and connection to the community disintegrates along with the devaluation of life itself that inevitability brings about the moral breakdown of society that gives rise to addiction, violence, marginalization of the poor, xenophobic hate mongering, and political polarization. This is the story of America's once prosperous communities and the descent of the people of America into "Trickle-Down" poverty in an America that now produces less than 4% percent of what it consumes.

The loss of America's industrial economic prosperity in the drive to create a subsistence-wage, debt-based casino economy, as Chris Hedges writes in *American Fascists*, "*turned ... most towns ... into a wilderness of poverty and urban decay ... Despair is the common denominator that shares a common feeling of loss, of abandonment, and deep pessimism about the future. When despair is this profound the desperate begin to seek miracles,*" welcome the "Man on a White Horse" with promises of prosperity for all. It becomes easier by the day to look for hope and comfort in the mystical hand."

As long as America's communities struggle to subsist in economic desperation, and the people of America remain demoralized and hungry in a financialized debt-based economy committed to wealth creation for a few, life for the many living in "quiet desperation" will remain polarized without purpose or meaning. The profiteers will continue to hunt down the poor; the hopes and cries of the helpless will gradually fade and die; and the "conspiracy of evil" will forever enslave a suffering People to the greed and corruption of the Conservative *"survival of the fittest"* world that destroys all who seek to be free.

The history of greed and power reminds us that a nation that denies its citizens the ability to earn a decent living from productive living-wage work is a nation bankrupt in moral and economic free fall. Is the reign of unhindered capital supremacy over a Republican politically engineered "surplus" people *"responsible for their own fate."* Is this to be the Conservative "survival of the fittest" America of the 21st Century? Are we to become an institutionalized "surplus" People of Liberty forever struggling to "make ends meet" in subsistence-wage serfdom?

Alexander Solzhenitzyn is said to have remarked that free people that take for granted their democracy would never surrender to totalitarianism. But tragically for America, the tyranny of greed did come to America to capture the soul of America, and in 1980 the Republican seizure of power that made for the "Pooring of America. And in 2016 and 2024, there sat in the shadows of inequity an authocrat on a "white horse" ready to promise "better times" to an abandoned "surplus" people - poor, desperate, and alone. That promise of better times, of course, like the 1980 Republican promise of "prosperity for all," would instead bring to America the meaning of "authoritarianism" and the making of dictatorship." This is the Conservative political reality that seeks to destroy American democracy through the corruption, lies, and disinformation of "designing Men." In the words of Abraham Lincoln, *"designing men" [who would] "destroy the government unless they be allowed to construe and enforce the Constitution as they please."*

I am reminded that Benjamin Franklin on hearing the comment, "We have a Republic," is said to have rejoined, *"If we can keep it."* I would think if Jean-Jacques Rousseau had been in the room he would have quipped, "of course, Franklin," "we may acquire liberty, but it is never recovered if it is lost." This is the terrifying and sober reality of American democracy today and our future as a People of Liberty.

IV

Rousseau was given to observe long before *"the worst of times"* of 1789, that *"democracy is not compatible with an excessive inequality of wealth."*

In the Coming of the French Revolution, French historian Georges Lefebvre points out the Revolution of 1789 was *"above all the conquest of equal rights."* The aristocrats of France in 1789 were the "tax exempt" predatory brokers of wealth, power and privilege of the country. They held absolute political-economic dominance over the land and the people. The ordinary people labored in a daily struggle to survive on a subsistence income obligated to bread, taxes, and rents. T*he demands of the people for systemic changes in 1789 were "the issues that caused the conflict to break out" - individual liberty, equal taxation, equality before the law, and political reform.* The people of the land who bore the burden of taxation in needless poverty *believed they should "be able to live on their work;" the standard of living should "be proportionate to their wages;" and government that gives a "free hand" to business and the aristocracy, should "take measures to assure the right of everyone to a living."*

Invoking the "rights of man," the people laid the foundation for the "Declaration of the Rights of Man and the Citizen" of 1789, which simply affirmed *"LIBERTY CONSISTS IN THE ABILITY TO DO WHATEVER DOES NOT HARM ANOTHER."*

Now in our desperate moment of subsistence-wage deprivation and desperation, we are a people given to feel the reality of the "Grim Reaper" authoritarian politics of "big money" "political extremism," excessive inequality of wealth, and the demise of America's "working" middle class majority. With the Republican fiscal policies of the last forty years directed to massive wealthy tax cuts, annual record budget deficits, and subsistence-wage labor, there is an evident parallel world between the predatory "Trickle Down" Conservative fiscal dominance over America today and the privileged French aristocracy of 1789.

The politics and privileges of both are the same with the same consequences. The average American worker is unable to make a decent living. Absent national political-economic reforms aimed at a livable-wage and a national fair and equitable tax policy, the Republican "feudal" tax policies of today, as with the French government of 1789, cannot *"raise by direct taxes revenue at all proportionate to the real wealth of the country,* or to its legitimate needs." That the French Revolution was necessary, Yale historian R.R. Palmer concludes, *"the old government simply failed to function, and its officials either would not or could not take the necessary measures necessary to maintain political life."*

V

As with the 1789 French political nightmare of aristocratic greed and entitlement, the Republican subsistence predatory political-economy has failed the American people. The working people of America subsist on pittance wages while a once prosperous America is at any given moment on the verge of economic collapse. Today the ashes of the Conservative ideological quagmire of Republican lies, scheming, and corruption, and today the advent of the Conservative "Project 2025," nullify any hope for a better America any time soon.

After decades of Republican abandonment and destruction of America's communities, jobs, and way of life, the people's day of reckoning showed itself in November 2020, as the people of America came together In desperation to cry out as did "David" long ago in a moment of national peril, greed, and corruption: *"The greedy hunt the poor … They mock their enemies … They delight in telling lies … All have become corrupt."* The political reality of 2025 is now the people's reality. As a People of Liberty we must be prepared in 2026 to deal with the challenges before us. With a renewed sense of community, we can redress as a People of Democracy in 2026 the painful Republican political abandonment of America, and return the land of Washington, Jefferson, and Lincoln to a nation of Freedom and Justice committed to the "general Welfare" and the "Blessings of Liberty" for all.

TODAY the Republican political establishment has "absolute power" to keep the people of America in "perpetual subjugation." In less than a year, Republican budgetary initiatives have funded $92 billion in corporate subsidies, $3.5 trillion in wealthy tax cuts, and, now, a $40 billion bailout for Argentina. Yet the Republican congressional majority has with zeal destroyed America's US AID international disaster relief program, slashed $300 billion from America's food assistance program, cut $1 trillion from Medicaid, established nation of concentration camps, and deployed the military in the streets of America. Republican autocracy TODAY rules over the "land of the free."

Now, America - BEWARE: "Project 2025" calls for the replacement of all income and corporate taxes with a "consumption" tax funded essentially by the working people of America. Yes, *only the little people pay taxes!*

And so, I ask, who do you say we are? Where do we stand as a People of Liberty as we approach the Election of 2026? Might we for a moment recount where the 50-year Republican political "assault on America" has brought us. The "conspiracy of evil" of the financial power elite in 1971, with the Powell Memorandum, enacted a comprehensive grand strategy to "save capitalism from democracy; in 1981, with Republican Trickle-Down Revolution, the Republicans embarked on a political crusade of wealth concentration and the pooring of America; and now, with the rise of the Conservative "Project 2025," the Republican 50-year "assault on America" is today ever present in a Republican "fascist" America of "every man for himself" in a Republican "survival of the fittest" America of "keep'em poor, keep'em sick, keep'em stupid."

This is the Republican power reality in this American moment. Is this, America, to be the Republican "autocratic" America of tomorrow our children and our grandchildren must inherit?

FOR
DEMOCRACY
TO
LET FREEDOM RING
EVERY VOTE MATTERS

LIBERTY IN FLAMES

Gone is our America of yesterday's middle
Class prosperity to Republican political and
Economic greed, corruption, and deceit

Lost is our America economically stable and
Secure in Liberty, Truth, and Justice to a
Conservative engineered financial debt-based
Casino economy of the *"survival of the fittest"*

No more is our America the once revered
"Beacon of Liberty" founded in Freedom and
Democracy pledged to protect "the general
Welfare" and the "Blessings of Liberty for
Ourselves and our Posterity"

Gone is our America of the "Rule of
Law" today politically deregulated to the
Predatory ideology of *"Profit over People,"*
Freedom from responsibility, Freedom
To starve" in a subsistence America of
"Every man America for himself"

DEMOCRACY ON FIRE

Louis Brandeis
Supreme Court Justice
*"The people of the United States are
now confronted with an emergency
more serious than war."*

MONDAY AFTERNOON

The Med-B-Crisis is spreading out of control while the indifferent politicians of the *"survival of the fittest"* administration refuse to respond with any collective action. *"People have to understand that healthcare is a matter of state policy; healthcare is everyone's individual responsibility."*

As Bob and Liz of the city's Crisis Response Unit engage in small talk, Liz looks up at Bob, "Something's on your mind, Bob?"

Bob smiles, "Nothing I can do anything about." "That sounds ominous," Liz replies. "Well, it's like this, Liz." "Last year the Republicans seized power through nationwide voter suppression laws, voter district gerrymandering, and a "dark money" radical campaign of lies and disinformation. Less than half of the American electorate went to the polls and the minority vote was the lowest in decades. Now, in less than a year, the Republicans have consolidated their "authoritarian" dominance over the country, raised taxes to pay for the new wealthy trillion dollar tax cuts, discontinued all family assistance programs, abandoned the infrastructure of assistance for the left behind, climate change control, and affordable healthcare.

Suddenly, a red alert call comes in for 13 Grace Avenue. Arriving at the scene they find a young woman lying unconscious on the pavement. Liz looks up at Bob: "Looks like RDX." Bob asks, "What's her Citizen Validation Quotient?" "Just a minute, "Liz says. "Ok, here we are, her CVQ reads: 'Marilyn Jones, Category 3 Sustainer, 32, divorced, two children, service worker, no healthcare coverage."

Bob, now resigned to the Conservative Individual Healthcare Protocol, says, "She'll have to go to the SEC (Surplus Euthanasia Center)." Liz, feeling numb, angrily responds, "We're taking this woman to the Hospital!" Visibly shaken, Bob walks slowly toward the emergency vehicle thinking to himself: 'NOW CALM DOWN! This is the reality of the new Republican "individual responsibility" healthcare system of "Creators, Producers, Sustainers, Freeloaders, and Parasites …"

"BUT THEN … when this crisis is over, LOOK OUT, over 30 million American workers will have permanently lost their jobs and health care coverage, the Hedge Fund and Private Equity raiders will race to clean out what remains of America's profitable small business ownership, the Investment Banks will fraudulently foreclose on millions of home mortgages, and the "predatory lenders" and "rent collectors" will come to life to scoop up the last dime and few possessions of the evicted and down and out. And what little remained of yesterday's America will be no more … Not really surprising, I guess … When the Roman Empire ceased to expand and there was finally no one left to plunder, the vultures turned inward to rob the masses and the state until the system just collapsed under the weight of corruption, duplicity, and betrayal. Well, here we go again."

II

The Constitution of these United States is a "living" promise of the people's rights that work only to the extent "We the People" are willing to support, protect, and defend that promise against all enemies both "foreign and domestic." By "domestic" is to say that in the shadows of wealth, power, and privilege "designing men" seek to hold political dominance over today's body politic and the wealth of America. It is here that history's most sober and cautionary saga reminds us that only a politically free sovereign people in control of their own political destiny can and will provide for the future freedom and prosperity of generations to come.

In the richest country in the world there is enough for every American to enjoy a productive, healthy, and peaceful life. In a representative democracy committed to a constitutional order that protects, promotes, protects, and defends the "general Welfare," the people are assured a share of the "blessings of liberty. Certainly it's not an attack on freedom as the proponents of "individual extremism" claim. IT IS FREEDOM!

President Theodore Roosevelt affirmed in an earlier desperate time: *"The only prosperity worth having" is that which affects the mass of the people … It is our duty to see that the wage worker, the small producer, the ordinary consumer…get their fair share of the benefit of business prosperity." "The most perfect political community" declared Aristotle, "is one in which the middle class is in control."* This is the meaning of America's greatness. This is the meaning of everything American coming together in democracy. The essence of the nobility and greatness of democracy is in the words of President Franklin Roosevelt: *"Government is ourselves the voters of this country."*

The daunting challenge before us is to prevent a Republican complete political takeover of American democracy by an authoritarian regime that seeks an American future of want, desperation, and despair, This is the urgent imperative of today's America as the desperation of everyday working Americans widens in the wake of the "Trickle-Down" monopoly inflationary assault on the people's cost of living.

The denial of state sponsored "Trickle-Down" human bondage in America can no longer be sustained. The ability to participate in America's prosperity in Freedom, Equality, and Justice are paramount if we are to feel the power of Liberty's promise. Most importantly, as citizens of democracy, we have duty and an obligation to follow the Truth, speak the Truth, and share the Truth.

Truth is the essence of who we are as a democratic people that empowers us as a *"sovereign people"* to be Forever Free. Freedom is Liberty's Truth. Democracy is Liberty's Trust. Equality is Liberty's Reality. Liberty is you and me walking the streets of America together in oneness regardless of who we are, the color of our skin, or where we came from. That we are the world's great *"melting pot"* of democracy is the nobility of what it means to be American. Our greatness is in what we are as a united People of Liberty Forever Free in a multi-ethnic, multicultural democracy. Liberty calls out of the darkness for the people of America to champion an America of Freedom, Equality, and Justice for all.

III

The Founder's promise of Liberty, Equality, and Justice is America's affirmation of Freedom, Democracy, and Truth. This is the founding promise upon which rests the idea of an America in which government is responsible to *"promote the "general Welfare, and secure the "Blessings of Liberty to ourselves and our Prosperity."*

To secure the Promise of Liberty for a just and inclusive America is the challenge before us. As Sylvia Clute notes in *Destiny Unveiled*, the task of restoration and renewal is straight forward: *"We must build a bulwark against governmental ... tyranny ... [and restore to America] ... a Nation that ... embodies Freedom ... Equality ... [and] the Masters Justice."* This sense of Liberty is the splendor, majesty, and glory of what Freedom represents to all the peoples of the world.

It is for each of us in this American moment to pledge as a People of Liberty our Faith, Loyalty, and Commitment to uphold and protect the Constitution of the United State against all enemies, "foreign and domestic."

What we are witnessing in this political moment is the "no holds barred" finale of the Republican end game *"to keep the common man in subjugation."* If history is any example, today's Conservative political extremism represents a radical turning point in the American experience. Remember it was the financiers and industrialists of central Europe that funded the "fascists" in exchange for docile workers and big profits. The "fascists" on assuming power in January 1933 dismantled the nation's democracy in the first six months of power.

And, in similar fashion, the Republican political establishment on assuming power in 1981,

> **IMPLEMENTED** the Conservative "Trickle-Down" Revolution; waged war on the workers' unions of America with Right To Work Laws;

DISMANTLED America's industrial prosperity to overseas cheap foreign labor;

DESTROYED America's ability to employ its people with secure living-wage jobs; and

ESTABLISHED the Conservative predatory "survival of the fittest" economy of *"every man himself."*

American democracy today is paralyzed from decades of Republican political greed, corruption, and political polarization. The very idea of America itself is in its final death throes. Unless democracy triumphs over the darkness of "fascist" greed, legal corruption, and political injustice in 2026, what remains of the idea of American democracy for future generations will not even be an historical footnote.

This is the national nightmare of this American moment as we bear witness to a new generation of "designing men" of "dark money" power corruption that is at the heart of the Conservative Social Darwin political-economic supremacy. The political reality here as we approach the coming 2026 election, as reported in *The Week* (December 2020): Republican candidates *"have shown … [a] willingness to use any means necessary to exercise power [in] that holding power is more important than preserving America's democracy."*

We must as a People of Liberty today we must understand the rise of American "fascism" for what it is, and what it represents for the future of democracy in America. As difficult as it may sound, consider we must the meaning of "radical rebellion" to comprehend the political reality of the Republican attempted violent takeover of democracy to seize absolute power. The people of America witnessed an armed violent revolutionary act causing death and destruction with the intent of political seizure of power on January 6, 2021. Remember this date. It will go down in the annals of the American experience as a "day of infamy," the crown jewel of American "fascism" that will forever enshrine the power of evil in our midst.

IV

Why the Republican Insurrection of January 6, 2021? The answer is "the leader" as Umberto Eco so powerfully writes in *Eternal Fascism*: he knows that his force is based on the weakness of the masses. The political dynamic in play is really very straight forward. "Fascism" is inherently racist, an ideology to mask resentment and hatred that puts money and power ahead of human beings. The fanatical despotism of "fascism" is *based on selective … qualitative populism. In a democracy … citizens have individual rights [and collectively] have a political impact … [in] the decision of the majority. For the "fascist", individuals as individuals have no rights, and the people are conceived as a quantity, a monolithic entity expressing the common will … Thus, the people is a theatrical fiction." And in that fiction there will come a future, where "a TV or Internet populist will present the emotional response of a selected group of citizens and be accepted as the Voice of the People.""*

The ultimate truth we are seeing is a reality few don't want to see, or perhaps, just don't want to believe can happen in America. *The seditionists "arrayed against American democracy,"*

Chris Hedges writes in *American Fascists*, *"hate the liberal, enlightened world formed by the Constitution [and]* "*are waiting for a moment to strike, a national crisis that will allow them to shred the Constitution ... bent on our destruction." "Power is not a means,"* writes Orwell, *it's "an end, the consequences" [of the] "act are included in the act itself."*

Is not any act that seeks to encourage, abet, or condone violent insurrection to obstruct a Constitutional transfer of power considered anarchy? Is not any act by any person, group, or party to limit, restrict, or hinder in any way the peoples' fundamental right to vote considered a criminal act? Is not any act by any government official, including members of Congress, that violates his or her Oath of Office to uphold, defend, and protect the Constitution of the United States a crime against the sovereignty of the people?

The ensuing reality following the attempted "fascist" coup d'état on the legislative branch of American governance may distract and confuse some. But we witnessed as a people the overwhelming majority of the Republican political establishment vote to block a bipartisan "Congressional Insurrection Commission." Time nevertheless has revealed the identity of those complicit in "the biggest threat to American democracy since the Civil War," from a corrupt "authoritarian" to the fomenters, perpetrators, the political terrorists themselves, and certainly all the Republican Congressional enablers having prior knowledge of the Republican plan to overthrow an officially elected United States Government. And with the outcome of the 2024 election, Republican power is absolute and all the participants in the insurrection have been pardoned.

In 2026 the political reality of "Democracy or Autocracy" is the political agenda. Parliamentary democracy in America is "on hold" through 2026 as the Republican political establishment holds the legislative power of "NO" over the "general Welfare" of the people. And be assured, the Republican power offensive in 2026 is to maintain absolute power to upend America's democracy. The Conservative "Project 2025" agenda is the 1930s racist authoritarian model of "fascism" for the future of America. Vice President Henry Wallace warned in a similar time, the American people to be awhere and understand America's "fascists" are the "designing men" of wealth and power who seek political power to *keep the common man in eternal subjugation.*

The lesson of the history of "fascism" is that a functioning democracy cannot withstand the march of "right-wing" extremism where there is a failure of democracy to hold politicians accountable and control anti-democratic disinformation, hate, and fear. American democracy in this American moment is in the hands of a Republican "fascist" political cabal committed to subvert the Constitution and grant Republicans in power the authority to negate Constitutional democracy in America. The death of Freedom and Democracy in America, and the hold of right-wing "fascist" authoritarianism forever in the hands of "designing men" is today on track to becoming reality.

Universal greed, political corruption, and the fundamental reality of "human bondage" now reign over the land of our fathers. All those days of yesterday's secure and prosperous way of life for a patriotic hardworking people are now all but a distant memory. The cornerstones of democracy have been slowly chipped away at to where the Constitutional right to express the will of the people has become a tarnished Republican "fascist" political mandate to enable power dominance. All that we once cherished as an American disappeared in a political instant in 1980, and today is the Republican world of political authoritarianism, legislative tyranny, district gerrymandering, and voter suppression.

The political reality of want, desperation, and despair in America today is the decades reality of the Republican "Trickle-Down" 1980 agenda to destroy the people's earning power and democratic way of life. Human life has become the Republican fodder of *"lives for profit"* enrichment to be enjoyed by the financial power elite at whatever the cost to democracy, to the people, to the nation.

The *"Republicans against Democracy"* struggle for the Soul of America threatens to forever erase America's traditions, values, culture of truth and human decency. Catherine Crier in Patriot Acts, discusses the political philosophy of Friedrich Hayek who has been often lauded by Conservative leaders in the 1980s. Crier reminds us that Hayek spoke of *"how political philosophy and personality coincide and the dangers this presents to a real democracy,"* and notes *"similarities between conservatives and socialists."* Conservatives do *"not object to coercion or arbitrary power.* **The Conservative believes "government … ought not to be too much restricted by rigid rules … [he's] content to expand government as long as they are in control … [and] like the socialist, he regards himself as entitled to force the values he holds on other people."**

V

Through hypocrisy, disinformation, and political deceit, radical Conservative extremism has gradually over four decades transformed America into a Republican subsistence debt-ridden casino society. This is no accident. The Republican "Pooring of America" of 1981 is the political foundation of despair that has brought open parochial "fascism" into the fray for Republican political dominance. Consider the "Pooring of America" in the context of the Republican four decade triumph of the 1981 Conservative "Trickle-Down" agenda. In 2026 we must remember how America became the Trickle-Down" society of want, desperation, and despair through,

> **Political Deregulation** of the "rule of law" in every sector of American life in pursuit of unhindered capital dominance over America that is today's "Trickle-Down" debt-based predatory economy, subsistence-wage living, monopolies, profiteers, climate change denial, and the concentration of America's wealth in the 1%;

> **Political Abandonment** of America's communities to overseas labor and big profits justified by the Conservative ideological extremism of "surplus" people are *responsible for their own fate";*

> **Political Erosion** of the ability of "representative" government to function on behalf of the "public good" in favor of the rich and the financial power elite;

Political Demise of truth, decency, and morality in the body politic through the ruthless employment of deceit, lies, disinformation, and the manipulation of democracy;

Political Suppression of state voter rights to disenfranchise millions of Americans from exercising the Constitutional right to vote and Republican engineered state election laws to reverse the "will" of the people;

Political Incitement of division, chaos, violence, and bloodshed to "overturn" the "will of the people" to maintain power supremacy and economic domination over America.

The "great storm" for the "soul of America" is upon us as "designing men" of greed and corruption endeavor to forever eradicate the promise of democracy that gives life to an America of "Liberty, Truth, and Justice.

Responsible leadership can bring about political change, but only through responsible Congressional legislation can change be accomplished. Today's Republican Congressional body of radical extremist politics will not support any meaningful people's initiative that will "promote the general Welfare" and the "common good" of the people. The Election of 2026 can be the new beginning for the return to an America of responsible representative government.

In a functional people's democracy, the essential reality of Equality and Justice is as President Franklin Roosevelt expressed during the "great depression" of the1930s: *"True individual freedom cannot exist without economic security and independence;*

freedom means the supremacy of human rights everywhere; our unity of purpose to gain those rights and keep them."

VI

The enormity of the tragedy of America's struggle to survive the Conservative predatory juggernaut can be readily understood once we consider America has the highest "poverty rate" among the Economic Cooperation and Development nations. The Conservative Social Darwin ideological *"survival of the fittest"* is today an illness that can bankrupt a family to a life of poverty, a college education is a guaranteed lifetime of student debt, and today's "bankrupt" retirees on Social Security struggle to exist a stone's throw away from life on the street.

Today's Republican legislated "Trickle-Down" policies are representative of the most extreme version of Social Darwin *"survival of the fittest"* economics. Political analyst Mike Lofgren, is want to remind us America *"ranks 35th (actually over 50th today) among the nations in life expectancy at birth."* And *"in measures of economic quality, social mobility, and poverty prevention, the United States ranks 27th out of the 31 advanced industrial nations ..."* The economic "Trickle-Down" reality of the Republican *"Profit over People"* predatory agenda is an America of devastated impoverished families struggling as "surplus people" on a subsistence living.

Professor Rana of the Cornell Law School writes: *"income and wealth inequality [has] dramatically increased ... social stagnation is increasingly the norm ...average earnings [are] barely above what they were 50 years ago; and 80% of the income growth [of recent years has gone] to the top 1%. "The silence,"* writes Michael

Steinberger in The Week (May 22, 2010), *"is yet another indication of how warped our politics [have] become."* The political disgrace of the Conservative political indifference and tragic non-response to America's national suffering is a national shame. In pure economic terms, at least 50 percent of America lives in poverty or on the edge of poverty. With an annual median per capita income at some $35,000, the real average hourly wage has stagnated since 1973; living-wage jobs are barely existent, and most employed Americans are in real time one pay check or medical crisis away from living on the street.

The social-economic devastation of the Republican predatory *"Profit over People"* subsistence world is for every working American the narrative of a suffering people abandoned and forgotten as "just surplus." We are a People of Liberty reliving the reincarnation of America's Gilded Age of devastating poverty, gargantuan wealth, absolute power and privilege, while the existence of a "surplus" people in crisis is committed to spending their entire subsistence bread, taxes, and rent. No one in America is poor because they want to be poor.

No one in America is homeless because they want be homeless. No one in America wants to die because they can't afford the medical procedure that will save their life. Some 180 million Americans across America live poor, desperate, or in fear of life itself because the Republican political establishment in the 1980s chose to "dance with the devil" to transform America's competitive free market economy and electoral democracy into a predatory debt-based "every man for himself" subsistence "animal farm" of unfettered profit and wealth concentration.

The four decade Conservative political-economic assault on America for power and wealth has delivered the American worker's middle class prosperity to the exploitation of the corruption of the speculators and profiteers. And the financial power elite, free of any obligations, have devastated all that we consider to be America, be it the rule of law, legislative oversight, income equality, affordable housing, healthcare and education, government services, and a family's right to prosper. We all hear or experience the voice of Salome in *"Why Is America Suffering:"* *"The way to destroy the family is to create such deep poverty that parents, working two or three jobs to survive ... lose touch with each other, and their children grow up as strangers."*

Wage poverty, human suffering, desperation, and despair are sufficient reasons we must confront in 2026 the financial greed, legal corruption, and political injustice of America's Conservative predatory *"Profit over People"* subsistence *"every man for himself"* America. The political outrage of America's national suffering is today who we are as a democratic people living manipulated, broken and discarded in an America once recognized as the "beacon of liberty."

To consume by fire is to obliterate all that is within the flames of destruction. This is the "Project 2025" strategic plan for America. America's Republican majority is laying the groundwork to consolidate absolute power over the people of America, destroy America's democratic institutions, and transform America into a "fascist" authoritarian state. The political reality before us, make no mistake, is we are in this American moment a "democracy on fire" about to be incinerated in the interest of concentrating power and wealth in the hands of the financial power elite.

The possibility for a new age of Freedom, Equality, and Justice is before us. The election of 2026 offers that one time opportunity in our life time to return America to the beliefs and values of the Founding Fathers to protect the "general Welfare" and the "blessings of liberty" for all the people. All depends now on the majority of the electorate having the moral courage to "accept [their] responsibility" *[to exercise]* "the right, the power, *and the duty to protect [their] own welfare."*

FOR
DEMOCRACY
TO
LET FREEDOM RING
EVERY VOTE MATTERS

POEM

SENSELESS MISERY

I see far and near the senseless
Misery of corruption, Political
Betrayal, and Racial Injustice

I bear the pain of an abandoned
"Surplus" people politically deceived,
Abandoned and Forgotten

I behold the hopelessness of a
Desperate mother's despair, the
Chains of the mass incarcerated

I share the inner quiet of a long
Suffering people longing for
Liberty, Truth, and Justice

HISTORICAL TRUTHS

"A house divided against itself cannot stand. I believe this nation cannot endure half slave and half free ... It will become all one thing or all the other."
President
Abraham Lincoln

The record shows that throughout history nations divided against itself are brought to destruction, and in most cases, as a direct result of an unrelenting greed for land, wealth, and power. America is a house divided, a nation embattled from Conservative lies and the disinformation of disruption that seeks to destroy American democracy in the name of unhampered capital supremacy, absolute power, and concentrated wealth.

The Conservatives of ideological extremism see themselves entitled to force the values they hold on other people to secure "unlimited government control."

We see not only the Republican promulgation of the "Big Lie" since the 2024 national election. We are now faced with a comprehensive Conservative attempt to "white wash" American history.

Consider we must the distasteful reality of "white supremacy" over America from the first days of the European invasion of the Americas in the 16th Century to the present moment. Racism is the hidden story of America from white settlement to the Civil War through Jim Crow America to the struggle for civil rights in the 1950s and 1960s. Today the Republican "white racist" racist campaign seeks to disenfranchise the minority vote and suppress Americans of color.

The Spanish in the 16th century conquered three empires in South America that reduced the native population from 25 million to 1.5 million. The English occupation of North America and America's "Manifest Destiny" march westward resulted in settler land grabs that forced the removal of the Amerindian population from their lands. By 1890 the native American population of 12 million was reduced to less than 300,000. Who today gives pause to reflect on the blood and sacrifice of the Trail of Tears, Sand Creek, or Wounded Knee?

In the English colonies of the 17th century, historian Abigail Swingen records in *Competing Visions of Empire*, *"blackness became equated with slavery, which had its starkest expression in colonial laws and codes [that] emphasized race in all matters. Race was the foundation of the social system; white skin meant freedom, domination, and power; black skin slavery, submission, and powerlessness … In a system that was based on oppressing the vast*

majority of the population … possessive individualism … valued
property rights above all else … Concepts of racial difference …
never ended for those who made it to the New World."

Who today knows of the ruthless oppression and suffering of Black Americans in America's enduring struggle to participate in an American "more perfect union? European and American serfdom, slavery, and exploitation continued as a divisive political exponent of American life to, and after, the Emancipation Proclamation of 1863. The reality of vulture colonialism at its peak witnessed two colonial powers controlling some 50% of the world. They murdered entire societies and looted their countries for 400 years. The occupation of India alone caused the deaths of over 60 million people.

In America, the "white supremacist" narrative has prevailed from the Reconstruction Era of racial segregation through the 1960s race struggle for "human rights" to present day America. And today the struggle for racial equality continues with the struggle against Republican voter suppression laws that are at the heart of the Conservative ideological "racial" doctrine to disenfranchise the minority vote from inclusion in the will of the majority.

President Johnson in 1965 signed into law the Voting Rights Act, legislation that was gutted by the Republican Conservative ideological "possessive individualism" that values property, wealth, and power above all else. The political reality of racism in this American moment is the bigotry, hatred, and advocacy for a "white supremacy" that is the personification of evil for all America.

The reality of the centuries old struggle for land, wealth, and white power need not distract from the "Idea of an America" envisioned by the Founding Fathers. Thomas Jefferson in 1776 drafted a clause in the Declaration of Independence condemning slavery, but was blocked by the southern slave interests over a required unanimous vote for Independence. From the beginning of the American experiment it was understood that the pursuit of Constitutional democracy of "liberty and justice for all" was going to be a never ending struggle toward a "more perfect union." To "white wash" American history is to deny the "Idea of America" and all who sacrificed, suffered, and died in the struggle for a "more perfect union."

Every American is entitled to an honest and meaningful understanding of America's history of "race and racism" however uncomfortable it may be for some. Racism is the reality of who we are as a people in this American moment. If we are to achieve the promise of a multiracial democracy of the world's exiles, we must address as a People of Liberty in 2026 the Conservative ideological "race" imperative that polarizes every aspect of American life.

The time has come we embrace together the promise our children pledge every day of an America of "liberty and justice for all." Despite the Conservative *"Assault on Democracy"* to achieve "white supremacy" over the body politic, the reality of who are as a People of Liberty in this American moment is captured so meaningfully by Heather McGhee, in *The Sum of Us: "We've found the enemy, and it's not each other."*

Now as I reflect on the "blessings of liberty" I've shared over a lifetime, I see our uniquely American beliefs about to be politically erased, and with it the beauty and majesty of what remains of all that we as a People of Liberty hold sacred: the liberty to worship, a democracy founded on Justice, civil liberties protected by the rule of law, every citizen's Constitutional right to vote, and the promise of a better tomorrow for all our children. With the passage of some 400 Republican voter rights suppression bills in 48 states, all that we cherish as a free democratic people is about to be transformed into a Republican "fascist" world of systemic oppression, national misery, and the despotism of individual powerlessness. This is America's ever-present "fascist" reality staring every American in the face."

A recurring Orwellian theme of totalitarianism is that "fascists" never assume power with the intention of relinquishing it. *"Are we dead,"* Orwell asks? *"Shall we meet in the place where there is no darkness?"* The answer avowed in the wisdom of President Franklin Roosevelt is *"democracy is not safe if the people tolerate the growth of private power."* Understand that private power is "fascism," the political authoritarian ownership of a people by a person of iniquity or by a small radical political establishment or oligarchy. And remember we must the warning of Sinclair Lewis to America: *"when fascism comes it will be wrapped in the flag and carrying a cross."*

The final battle for America has begun. We are a country in this American moment facing the ultimate reality of political truth that authoritarian rule is the death of a nation. To recognize and resist this fundamental reality in any democracy, the question before a People of Liberty becomes, at what point does a democratic nation declare a radicalized political "party" committed to the "overthrow of democracy" a criminal organization.

For a People of Liberty who Pledge Allegiance to a free Democratic Republic and a culture of "liberty and justice for all," it is an unimaginable human tragedy to see over 180 million Americans struggling to subsist in a "fascist" world of the *"survival of the fittest,"* when over a million Americans have given their "last full measure" on a thousand battlefields in the belief of an America of Freedom, Equality, and Justice "forever free."

While Republicans have been able to unanimously vote to block legislation for infrastructure renewal, family assistance, and job initiatives, legislation in the interest of the "common good" has shown that determined and timely government intervention is paramount to the preservation of the life of the nation. The "democratic people's agenda was in every sense a one-time road to national recovery for a people where the top 1% of income earners have a greater share of household wealth than the whole of middle class America. At a cost of 1.2% of GDP, *The Week* (October 22, 2021) reports that the passage of human infrastructure legislation is essential to addressing America's "alarming stagnation" and "soaring economic inequality." The legislation would address care for the elderly, investment in public education, and combat climate change. "Child tax credits will lift millions of children out of poverty," reduce prescription drug bills costs for seniors, and strengthen working American families. Writes journalist Dave D'Alessandro of the Newark *N.J Star-Ledger: "Every year we fail to invest in kids and education leads to continuing poverty and 'decades of wasted human potential.' If we don't invest in the future, our future will be grim."*

As America's democratic national recovery effort flounders from Republican predatory political destruction, the challenge before us in 2026 must focus on the resolve, resilience, and perseverance of Truth, Democracy, and Justice if we are to achieve a new era of "Liberty, Equality, and Justice for all."

FOR
DEMOCRACY
TO
LET FREEDOM RING
EVERY VOTE MATTERS

FREEDOM

How sweet the sound of Liberty
It soothes our sorrows, heals our
Wounds, and drives away our fears

Our strength is in the things we
Value: Truth, Equality, Justice,
Family, Dignity, and Respect

The time is now we assert who
We are: either we are a People
of Liberty ... or
WE ARE NOTHING!

A PLANET IN CRISIS

"Climate change is one of the gravest crisis our planet has ever faced." The "most important lawsuit on the planet" was filed in 2015 in the U.S. District Court of Eugene, Oregon. The federal court judge ruled the case to go forward, saying: "I have no doubt that to a right to a climate system capable of sustaining human life is fundamental to a free and ordered society. Public trust rights "both predated the Constitution and are secured by it, and can't be "legislated away."
David Russell
Horsemen of the Apocalypse

MONDAY EVENING

In the quiet of late evening, Bill and Martha relax in conversation on the latest destructive disaster of an America in permanent political-economic crisis.

85

With a blank expression of foreboding, Bill asks, "What's that line, 'water, water everywhere'? Martha, seeing Bill is anxiously pondering the day's consequences of the unrelenting Conservative denial of Climate Change, says "that would be Samuel Taylor Coleridge's *The Ancient Mariner,* "Water Water everywhere not a drop to drink." Perhaps the plight we may all face in the very near future. Why do you ask?"

"Just a lingering thought. Martha, on the latest catastrophic flooding along the East and Gulf Coasts: "water everywhere," billion dollar infrastructure devastation, and the loss of power for over a million people. I'm afraid, Martha, this is the new normal for humanity and the planet. Climate change and environmental disaster is here, and it's hitting hard this year everywhere across the planet.

"The Conservative apologists of political *"survival of the fittest"* extremism don't want to hear the oceans are warming, or the world's glaciers are disappearing as a consequence of global carbon pollution. And they even refuse to acknowledge the Climate Change reality that each new year is becoming the hottest year on record. Devastating hurricanes, typhoons, droughts, flooding, firestorms, and earthquakes are raining havoc and destruction on every continent. Seventy percent of the planet's forests have been cut down, altering the ecological balance of the Earth, eight million animal and plant species on the planet are on the threshold of extinction, and Planet Earth is projected to be on the road to environmental collapse by 2050.

"The global climate apocalypse of destruction, Martha, is the carbon energy reality before us as we continue to produce over 85 billion tons of carbon emissions annually. Sea levels are rising; power grids overwhelmed; water reservoirs depleted; infrastructure burning. The last ten years have been the warmest on record. The 2021 heat wave broke record highs in South America, the United States, Canada, England, Europe, and Asia. The decade-long drought in America's Southwest is on a path to be the worst in 1,200 years. The catastrophic flooding in Germany, Turkey, and China is the worst in a century.

And now Martha, I see *The Week* (December 8, 2023) reports that "November 17, 2023 ... was the first day in human history when the average global temperature hit 2 degrees Celsius warmer than pre-industrial levels ... Every month since June has set a new high temperature ... Earth is speeding toward a record warming of 2.5 to 2.9 degrees Celsius by the end of the century."

Time is running out for Planet Earth as the Republican "dark money" anti-climate profit agenda continues to block Congressional action to fund Global Warming control through a measured public policy that would transform America's fossil fuel dependency to a 21st Century American Renewable Clean Energy Infrastructure. The climate change crisis of global carbon pollution is for a burning planet the most deplorable *Lives for Profit* "collateral damage" event in human history. As the planet heats up destroying lives, property, and infrastructure, America's Republican *"survival of the fittest"* fossil fuel gurus of climate change denial and "dark money" politics have politically rolled-back America's environmental protections, abandoned climate change agreements, and blocked cheap renewable energy initiatives.

"I understand, Bill. But through the political control of power corruption, the Conservative political extremists have been able to TRANSFORM our once national economic prosperity into a profit apocalypse of impoverished serfdom, hunger, and want; FOSTER a violent insurrection to overturn America's democratic electoral process to maintain power; DISENFRANCHISE millions of citizens from their Constitution right to vote; and REORDER with impunity a national pandemic into a Republican political homicidal apocalypse that gave us over a million deaths. That begs the political reality before us in 2026: Can our battered democratic institutions protect the people's Constitutional safeguards designed to defend American democracy from enemies not only "foreign," but enemies "domestic?"

The challenge of Climate Change destruction is as you often fume, Bill. The story of politically protected profit supremacy over planetary sustainability. Despite the annual increase of catastrophic climate events throughout the world in number, frequency, and intensity, the "big money" power brokers of climate change denial control the politics of unhindered vulture capitalism, climate change legislation, and clean energy.

"I would say that sums up the reality of the Conservative authoritarian "dark money" politics of the *"survival of the fittest"* capital supremacy in America, Martha. America's

Conservative environmental reality is the destruction of the planet to satisfy an insatiable craving for wealth and profit over human life itself. It's the Republican Fifty-Year extremism of *"Profit over People"* at whatever the cost to humanity and the environment all over again.

"Just follow the money, Martha. Wealth and profit are at the heart of the political debate over Climate Change. Conservative Climate Change denial is about "big money" power blocking any people's initiative for reducing the carbon blue print and clean energy renewal. It's about "profit over people" in a "survival of the fittest" world of billion dollar "fossil fuel" profits. It's about the financial power elite restricting any means for giving a People of Liberty hope to live without struggle and suffering. It's about protecting the profits, wealth, and privilege working to prevent "sweeping historical changes" that will mandate the Ultra-Rich pay something instead of nothing, or for opening a can of worms that could mandate living-wage jobs that will strengthen working families with affordable housing, child care, and education."

"I know, Bill. But this is our Conservative ideological "survival of the fittest" political-economic reality. Even though "73% of Americans support policies to cut greenhouse gas emissions in half by 2030," the destructive political power of greed and corruption holds us and our planetary world hostage to unfettered climate exploitation. There's no alternative to mankind's reconciliation with creation. Earth's reality for our climate "destruction" denial is about to come to fruition. And, it's coming sooner than we think!"

"But I have hope, Bill. Light will emerge from the darkness. And our fading democracy will be transformed once again into a land of the living. Greed and corruption will be swallowed up in victory over the corrupting evil of concentrated wealth. And the sting of death that now imperils the people of America in every sphere of American life will be no more. I know, Bill, it's wishful thing, but without some climate action there will be no livable planet for future generations."

"In our quest for Liberty, Democracy, and Freedom, Martha, we do *"have it in our power to begin the world over again."* "Political change for the survival of the "common good" and the future of the planet comes down to who and what we vote for: people who support an Autocracy of Exploitation or a Democracy that protects the people and the planet."

Look around Children of the Earth, the planet mourns, *"as the Land lies polluted, defiled by its inhabitants who have transgressed the laws … a curse consumes the land and its people."*

FOR

DEMOCRACY

TO

LET FREEDOM RING

EVERY VOTE MATTERS

POEM

A WORLD DEFILED

I feel the raging fury of
Betrayal and corruption
Ravaging a world defiled

I weep for the many struggling
the desperation of unchecked
climate destruction

I behold with compassion
A planet longing for clean
Energy in a burning world

FOREVER WAR

*"In time of war the
first casualty is truth"*

*"The biggest farce of
man's history has been the
argument that wars are fought
to save civilization"*

*"In time of war
the rich get the shekels
and the poor get the shackles"*

SUNDAY EVENING

Bill, rising from his chair before the television with a sigh of disgust mutters to himself, "The 20-year $300 million a day Afghan War is over. But is the golden goose that never stops giving really dead?"

"What's that? Martha calls out. Walking into the sitting room with a smile, she asks, "What was that all about?"

"I was just commenting to myself on the fall of Afghanistan, Martha. We've ventured to engage in a twenty year military-economic deployment in Asia, Africa, and the Middle East on a "credit card." That has involved six wars, and all that remains are the remnants of "delusion and dishonesty," over a million dead, countries destroyed, displacement, and hunger numbering over 30 million as displaced human beings flee the chaos of devastation and destruction. And, of course, there's the $8 trillion war debt with over $2 trillion in interest that will never be paid off in our lifetime." America has engaged in 15 military interventions over the last 42 years, and whenever a "petty dictator" or "Jihadist" flexes a muscle, or an American "imperialist" craves another country's natural resources, the Conservative politicians, foreign policy groups, and political action committees, backed by right-wing money and influence, agitate for intervention."

"The 20-year Afghan War is no different than the Vietnam War triggered over a dubious incident, the Iraq debacle waged over weapons of mass destruction that didn't exist, and so many other tragic interventions of 'imperial' overreach. And after a year or so when the conflict becomes a "forever war," no one can explain why that in the end benefits only the "flag waving" political "war profiteers" and the coffers of the financial-industrial complex. Already, the political flag of righteousness is flying anew for war. It never ends, Martha, power and profit at whatever the cost marches on to the tune of deceit and destruction just as the prophet Ezekiel of long ago proclaimed, "They have seduced my people, saying, "Peace!" when there is no peace."

"Well, Bill, what it comes down to as George Orwell makes clear, "*War is not to be won. It is meant to be continuous.*" I would think what it really comes down to in a democracy is who the people vote for, the candidate who values "people over profit" and a sense of humanity, or those who advocate the Conservative "survival of the fittest" extremism of unhampered vulture capitalism at any cost."

"Yes, Martha, that's the answer for a democratic people free of unaccountable "dark money" politics that has within its grip the ability to control the people's destiny and the future of American democracy. But think about it for a moment. "War" is something we rarely talk about unless there is an incident somewhere in the world involving the loss of American lives. War is the least discussed topic in American politics. No one is willing to acknowledge the business of war is the most profitable business of unrestricted capital supremacy."

"Actually, Martha, I see the real reason we pulled out of Afghanistan is we are simply a bankrupt nation. The unhampered supremacy of capital has destroyed America and the promise of democracy. The American empire is in its death throes. America's hegemony over global profits can no longer be sustained. The inflated dollar, massive borrowing, and rising federal deficits over the last five decades that have funded America's informal "imperial" expansion around the world has come to an end. Decades of waging war on a credit card, trillion dollar bank bailouts, decades of recurring wealthy tax cuts that didn't pay for themselves, billions in annual corporate subsidies, printing money at will, and our casino economic system have all contributed to America's decline since the 1981 Republican "Trickle-Down" Revolution of deregulation and private wealth creation, and today's $36 trillion national debt primarily driven by Republican greed and political malfeasance."

"This all becomes relevant, Martha, when we understand America's wealth today is concentrated in the top 1% that owns more wealth than the people of America. The wealthiest among us and the richest corporations pay little to no taxes, while over two-thirds of everyday working Americans subsist on a low-wage income in which over 90% goes to food, rent, and taxes You would think with the trillions of dollars we spend on killing people, we could find the money to help America's "surplus" left behind."

"The fiscal reality of America is we're broke, Martha. And that's not just you and me and the neighbor next door. America is broke. We no longer can sustain wealthy trillion dollar tax cuts and billions in corporate subsidies any longer without massive borrowing. All this business of war seems as John Lanchester observed recently in the *London Review of Books*, *'We have in effect had to declare war to get us out of the hole created by our economic system.'*" Now, that may sound somewhat ridiculous, Martha, but I have a feeling we are about to go to war for just that reason."

"I understand, Bill. But I find this all disgustingly pathetic, repulsive, and disheartening. I just don't see any legitimacy in conflicts of death and destruction waged in our name to make the world safe for profiteering. The hard truth of American politics is that the vast majority of the American people neither grasps nor subscribes to the flagrant corruption and manipulation of the politics of exploitation. In fact, most Americans show little concern for day-to-day policy issues and are prone to accept party line disinformation. The triumph of greed at any cost is just not who we are, Bill, or what the Framers intended for an America founded on the idea of Liberty, Truth, and Justice."

"What we are witnessing Bill, both at home and around the world is a catastrophic human apocalypse involving millions of human beings struggling to survive hunger, forced migration, and political repression. And this, in one way or another, is the unfortunate tragic consequence of our domestic politics of greed, decades of foreign policy failures, and forever-wars of profit, death, and destruction.'"

"When I look in the mirror, Bill, I see the distant quagmires of Vietnam, Afghanistan, and Iraq, and an America of bankrupt impoverished communities, their people made "surplus" and destitute in the quest for profit. I see the reflection of an America in crisis, an America broken, lonely, and hurting, and a struggling people who surely understand the frailty of just being human in an unjust predatory world of reckless greed, shameless corruption, and political betrayal. But most of all, Bill, I still see that see we are a People of Liberty who cherish from the depths of our being the inviolability of an American democracy that protects and defends for one and all 'the Blessings of Liberty."

"While reading *The Week* news the other day, I came across a report that cited 85% of Americans when surveyed declared themselves to be Christian. Given the reality of the Republican Conservative principles of the *"survival of the fittest, a "people responsible for their own fate,* and the labeling of the "left behind" as "surplus" people to be abandoned and forgotten is inconceivable in an America of "Liberty and Justice for All."

"Doesn't anyone remember anymore, Bill, George Washington stressed that religion and morality were the abiding principles of the nation; Thomas Jefferson asserted *"all men are created equal" "endowed with certain inalienable rights: "life, liberty, and the pursuit of happiness;"* James Madison affirmed "the Bill of Rights" sought to protect every American to the fullest, and Justice Earl Warren believed the Bill of Rights came into being to secure "freedom of belief, of assembly, of petition, the dignity of the individual, the sanctity of the home, and equal justice under the law.'"

"With all what is going on with the autocracy of Republican governance, as a Christian I need to feel the 'essence of being' that Chris Hedges writes so powerfully in *The World As It Is.* The 'essence of being" being a love that embodies what freedom and democracy are meant to represent. A love that recognizes the *"sanctity of all human beings ... allows us to embrace and cherish life ... to cope with [the]inevitable despair and suffering [of the people] in the healing solidarity of kindness, compassion, and self-sacrifice ... resist in our nature what we know we must resist and affirm what we know we must affirm ... [to] acknowledge that to love another as one loves oneself is to love the universal self that unites us all ... gives us meaning that endures ... and alone can save us, especially from ourselves.'"*

"American Exceptionalism to me, Bill, means we are a People of Liberty gathered in the world's greatest "melting pot" of democratic freedom, a nation of "malice toward none" that out of the many we are one united in a lasting social order that itself bears witness to America's founding values of Liberty, Truth, and Justice. This is what the Founders meant we must become in the pursuit of "a more perfect union," a People of Liberty sharing values in a nation that embodies the meaning of democracy in an America dedicated to 'Liberty and Justice for All.'"

"Today everywhere we look, we bear witness to the reality we are a "Trickle-Down" People of Liberty stranded in a Republican desert of want, desperation, and despair. Nevertheless, despite all our flaws, Bill, and all the political injustices carried out by the power brokers in our name, we are a resolute people constitutionally committed *"In God We Trust"* to an America of Democracy, Truth, and Justice. These are troubled times that endeavor to radicalize and blind the uninformed to the Republican campaign of lies, disinformation, and deceit that only subverts the essence of American freedom and democracy. The tyranny of wealth and power of "designing men" as Daniel Webster forewarned, threatens in this American moment all we hold sacred as a People of Liberty. One day the darkness of greed and corruption that seeks to eliminate the "Blessings of Liberty" will be over. It is now for all who celebrate Liberty in America's "darkest hour" to give hope to those who have none."

"'Courage,' the Roman playwright Plautus reminds us, *"is what preserves our liberty, safety, life, and homes and parents, our country and children."* As a People of Liberty we must stand firm in truth, embrace the freedom of our fathers, and be strong and courageous for an America "forever free." This, Bill, is our only hope, not just today, but for an American democracy for all generations to come."

FOR
DEMOCRACY
TO
LET FREEDOM RING
EVERY VOTE MATTERS

POEM

PEACE SAY WE

"PEACE" Say We
to the
Power Brokers of
Greed

"PEACE" Say We
to the
Merchants of
Death

"PEACE" Say We
to the
Predatory Wars of
Human Suffering

DESPERATE LIVES

EARLY MORNING

Frank looks over at Mary, "You're not saying much this morning, Mary?" Mary, pale and visibly tired, says, "Well, I'm here. What can I say? I'm working three jobs for nickels and dimes. My girls are sick without adequate medical care. And I'm never sure we're going to make it to month's end."

Jen speaking with an air of assuredness begins, "Something's got to give guys! All there is here is crumbling roads, rusting factories, discount strip malls, franchise restaurants, box stores, and abandoned people *"responsible for their own fate."* And "white nationalist" Republican politicians block any productive meaningful proposal that will benefit the "common good." That is, of course, except for the grift, tax cuts, and subsidies for the common good of the top 1%."

Bob breaks in, "Here she goes again. She's frustrated because she reads too much." "Actually," Frank rejoins, "she is in fact more often right than not." Jen, excited now, looks at Bob, and begins, "Bob, you just don't get it. You just don't want to hear the truth. All you listen to is conspiracy theories, disinformation, and the politics of individual extremism that enable poverty, forever debt, death care, and like my neighbors, old age on the streets."

All began to speak at once. "OK guys!" Frank says. "Just what do you feel is the truth, Jen?" With a hard look on her face, Jen says pointedly, "After decades of Republican "Trickle-Down" lies and deceit there's simply nothing left. Downtown America is an empty shell. Small business ownership barely exists. Extreme wealth owns everything. Regulatory restraint and accountability are dead. Catastrophic climate change devastation is here. Our secure living-wage jobs have gone south. Old age pension security for the elderly is gone! And the Republicans relentlessly pursue the destruction of the democratic state and their *"survival of the fittest"* ideological obsession to privatize Social Security, Medicare, and public education, and eliminate minimum wage laws."

"Look around you. It gets worse. Costs continue to rise without wage relief. People are hurting. Families are struggling. Children are hungry. The struggle to maintain a decent place to live has become an everyday reality. Nobody really has anything but cheap toys. There is little to no opportunity for our children to work for a better life. And homelessness across America has become the people's scourge of America's 21st Century."

"Who remembers today when the Republicans embraced "white supremacy" paranoia and extreme political divisiveness, and enacted trillion dollar wealthy tax cuts, added trillions to the Federal deficit? Who among us took issue with the Constitutional lawlessness when the Republicans passed nationwide racial based state voter suppression laws, blocked a self-funded 3.5 trillion dollar national human and physical infrastructure package to address poverty, good paying jobs, roads and bridges, child care, housing, and climate change initiatives to build an equitable America for all the people? Who among us stood up to condemn the horror of the "unanimous" Republican vote to "gut" the National the Voting Rights Act designed to save American democracy from the hypocrisy of "fascism"? Sadly, the answer is staring us in the face as we, a People of Liberty, bear witness to the everyday inequality and injustices of the Republican "Trickle-Down America of want, desperation, and despair"

"OK, Jen, so what's the answer, Bob asks? I know you guys don't want to talk politics," Jan responds, "but the first step is to acknowledge the Republican political reality for what it is. Then and only then can we begin to bring about change." Everybody nods in somewhat agreement.

"The truth is," Jen continues without so much as a breath, "we each bear in our own way the political human bondage of the Republican "Trickle-Down" economy of shame: insecure work, service jobs, pauper wages, unaffordable healthcare, housing, and education, and a subsistence standard of living. Think about it for a moment, rampant gun violence dominates our lives, opportunity for our children's future is all but non- existent, legalized financial corruption has control over the economy, and the nation's wealth and economic growth goes to the top 1%. We see every day the Republican racial extremism of "Jim Crow" racial oppression, intimidation, and the Republican denial of every American's Constitutional right to vote. Face it, the people's America of the "Land of the Free" is a wholly owned subsidiary of the financial power elite controlled through Conservative "dark money," domination by an authoritarian political establishment of legislative obstruction, and the spread of Republican lies, disinformation, and deceit."

"Now, if we are really serious about restoring the "Land of the Free" to a democracy "of the people," we must today call out as a People of Liberty the the reality of the REPUBLICAN CONSERVATIVE CULTURE OF DEATH:

ENVIRONMENTAL GENOCIDE is Climate Change "denial" as an expedient of the "Politics of Profit" over Human Existence;

HUMAN BONDAGE is the politically authorized "Profit over People" debt-based "subsistence" economy of state sponsored unaccountable "dark money" electoral dominance;

POLITICAL GENOCIDE is the "peoples' coming apocalypse" given the reality of the Conservative "Project 2025" goal to marginalize the elderly, the disabled, the poor and the homeless.

POLITICAL LIBEL is the proliferation of lies, disinformation, and deceit to undermine Constitutional democracy;

POLITICAL MANSLAUGHTER is the dissemination of Covid anti-vaccine lies and disinformation as an expression of radical ideological extremism;

POLITICAL TYRANNY is the political obstruction of Constitutional governance, be it executive, legislative, or Conservative higher court bias;

STATE FASCISM is the Republican state "voter suppression" laws and state election appointees authorized to overturn the "will" of the people;

TREASON in any country is the reality of a violent political insurrection to overthrow a legitimate election for all involved regardless of status, position, or influence.

WHITE SUPREMACY hate speech and racial injustice in today's context is what Hannah Arendt referred to as "THE BANALITY OF EVIL;"

"We must face the reality we are a People of Liberty who've been transformed by decades of Conservative power dominance from a 1970s industrial nation of "prosperity for all" to the 1980s Republican Financialized "Trickle-Down" Society of the *survival of the fittest* and the Pooring of America, to the collapse of a once prosperous middle-class. The nation is polarized and divided, public values and morality have withered, and now, in this American moment, we are a People of Liberty living the reality of an unstable politically compromised democracy on the verge of disintegration through the Republican "Project 2025" agenda."

"The Republican 1971 offensive of political "betrayal" of America to "save capitalism from democracy" is today a Conservative America of subsistence wages, unaffordable cost of living, and an abandoned "surplus" democratic people struggling to survive the fascistism of "dark money" political corruption."

"So, in answer to your question, Bob, the solution to greed and corruption in American politics is very straight forward:

> LEGISLATION that ensures the unencumbered universal right to vote with the assurance every vote will be counted without political partisan interference;

> CAMPAIGN FINANCE REFORM that prohibits campaign "dark money" financing; and

> FEDERAL OVERSIGHT ACCOUNTABILITY legislatively mandated to regulate finance, business, and politics regardless the political party in power.

"Given today's tragic reality of disinformation, lies, and deceit in the body politic, political parties, politicians, and broadcasters must be held responsible under penalty of law to uphold the veracity of truth. Freedom of speech doesn't give anyone in a democracy the right to destroy or to malign, disparage, or defame, regardless who is in power ..."

"The time has come we address as a People of Liberty the "Banality of Evil" in our midst. Freedom is the Constitutional Right to Vote for every American. Every citizen's vote is the Life Blood of American democracy. I would think even you, Bob, would acknowledge that any "extremist" party that advocates white supremacy, racial voter suppression, electoral subversion, elector certification fraud, violent insurrection, subsistence-wage servitude, and the deregulation" of laws that assure a fair and just society is a "criminal organization."

"If "We the People" are to once again prosper in a secure stable democracy of Liberty, Truth, and Justice, Theodore Roosevelt reminds us that we, as a People of Liberty, *"have the right, the power, and the duty to protect [ourselves] and [our] own welfare" from the servitude of "human bondage."*

Frank, looking at his watch with a smile, stands to announce, "OK everybody, it's time to go."

II

America's Profit over People predatory "Trickle-Down" economy of wealthy tax elimination, big business "zero" taxation, subsistence-wage jobs, Lives for Profit healthcare, and middle class retirement poverty has today impoverished millions of Americans. The reason is the Conservative political-economic supremacy over America's electoral democracy, achieved by the "political economy" theories of Buchanan, Friedman, and Bork, the Powell strategic grand design to "save capitalism against democracy," and two Conservative Supreme Court "dark money" decisions.

As a consequence of the Supreme Court's rulings in Buckley 1976 and Citizens United 2010, the triumph of the Republican "Trickle Down" agenda through aggressive "big money" vested interest financing, empty promises, and political disinformation, the Conservative "big money" political initiative in the end delivered the demise of the America's competitive free market economy and the making of the Republican predatory *"Lives for Profit"* subsistence America.

The political-economic reality of the Conservative Fifty-Year Republican campaign to *"save capitalism from democracy"* is an America of wealth creation for a few, and for everybody else a life of economic bondage and desperation in an America lacking economic security, livable-wages, safe working conditions, affordable healthcare, and a society safe to raise a family.

The 1971 Powell strategic political grand design for achieving Republican political dominance over the American people in the 1980s, created America's financialized debt based casino economy of *"Profit over People"* ideological extremism advanced by Buchanan, Friedman, and Bork. The underlying political reality of the Republican "Trickle-Down" Revolution has been an all encompassing transformation of American democracy into a Conservative impoverished world of economic servitude, political moral depravity, and unhampered capital supremacy.

The Conservative ideological extremism of absolute power and wealth creation is today's America.

Chris Hedges in *The World As It Is,* observed today's America of "unchecked greed" is the working persons' struggle to survive in a Conservative playground of exploitation and profit that sees ***"EVERYTHING FROM HUMAN BEINGS TO THE NATURAL ENVIRONMENT AS EXPLOITABLE COMMODITIES."***

The predatory Conservative "every man for himself" America is today the political triumph of the Republican decades-long "deregulation" offensive of market manipulation, financial growth gimmicks, and the demise of middle class America. However politically disguised, it is the Republican cornerstone reality of the Republican *"survival of the fittest"* ideology of the Conservative Social Darwin political economy of political dominance.

II

The Republican political triumphs of 1980, 1994, 2010, and 2016, provided impetus for the Republican political establishment to freely engage in a concentrated "assault against democracy" through the enactment of the Republican "Trickle-Down" economic agenda: the destruction of America's competitive community-based industrial economy to a predatory consumer debt-based wilderness of monopolists, profiteers and financial speculators.

The Republican "deregulation" of America's competitive free market economy championed by the Milton Friedman "myth" of uncontrolled self-adjusting free markets paved the way for an America of rusting factories, bankrupt communities, and a predatory financialized debt-based casino economy of part-time subsistence-wage labor. The Republican abandonment of the Sherman Antitrust Act through therevision or abandonment of anti-trust regulations provided the capstone for the triumph of the Bork Doctrine to *"allow firms to achieve available efficiencies through mergers without interference."*

With the Republican legislated "deregulation" of government accountability oversight of the financial industry and subsequent repeal of the Glass-Steagall Act of 1935, the people of America lost all consumer and banking protection from the investment profiteers of financial growth gimmicks, and the derivatives speculation debacle that facilitated the 2007 great housing-bubble meltdown and the "2008 Financial Collapse." And it was the Republican legislated "deregulation" of the finance industry that provided the trigger for America's "financial collapse" that wiped out millions of jobs, people's life savings, retirement pension accounts, and millions of home owners to foreclosure fraud, as the moneylenders, speculators, and profiteers were protected from criminal prosecution and received taxpayer funded trillion dollar government bailouts.

III

It should come as no surprise that over half of the population of America anguishes everyday on why their children are hungry, why they are working two and three jobs and still can't get a head of their situation. Every American should be asking how it is, as a People of Liberty, good hard working people in the richest country in the world are caught up in a political quagmire of want and desperation, fleeced of yesterday's opportunities to prosper, and struggle ever day of their lives in a Conservative engineered *Lives for Profit* predatory "Trickle-Down" subsistence economy.

In pure economic terms, all of America's economic gain over the last three decades has gone to the top, over 50% of Americans' live in poverty or on the edge of poverty, or just homeless. With an annual median per capita income at some $35,000, the real hourly wage has stagnated since 1973; Millions of American workers long for a non-existent living-wage job, and most employed Americans are in real time one pay check or medical crisis away from living on the street.

Economic stagnation, family consumer debt, and "forever" student debt is America's national norm of some 18 trillion dollars in consumer debt that includes $1.5 trillion dollars in forever student debt. In 2019, America's overall debt rose to 102% of GDP, the national debt exceeded $22 billion and now in 2025 is at $36 trillion, principally due to several wealthy trillion dollar tax cuts, moneylender speculation bailouts, and decades years of unending credit card funded foreign wars.

An impoverished America of more than 180 million urban and rural working poor struggle to cope with the basic necessities of life. Average earnings for the American worker are barely what they were 50 years ago while the median annual income for two income households remains stagnant at some $58,000, two out of three working Americans earn less than a living wage, while 75%t of Americans live paycheck to paycheck never knowing when the next paycheck will be the last. Two-thirds of the American people have less than $1,000 in savings, while 44 percent of Americans don't have $400 in available cash for an emergency. The ten million Americans who can't access the banking system are the fodder of the predatory loan-shark pay day lenders that prey on the working poor.

The average America worker lives on a subsistence income with monthly expenditures of $2000 to $2500 for rent, $1300 in child care, and outrageous "inflated" monopoly food, medicine, and transportation costs. And now in 2026 we find middle income families faced with "a cost of living crisis" from the Republican tariff wars, ballooning rents, sky-rocketing child care, spiraling healthcare, and prohibitive educational debt in the struggle to just survive. This is all taking place as America's financial institutions individually gross more than $40 billion in annual profits while the Ultra-Rich and two thirds of America's top corporations pay little to no federal income tax.

Certainly food is the basic human need. Since the advent of the Republican "Trickle-Down" Revolution of the 1980s, homelessness, hunger, and malnutrition have mushroomed across America as factories closed, jobs disappeared to low-wage countries, and Americans subsisted under the Conservative Social Darwin ideological policies to maximize profits. And in the richest country in the world, over 50 million Americans today live hungry, another 20 million Americans live malnourished, some 20 percent of America's children go to bed hungry, and one in two children in their childhood years need food assistance to alleviate nutritional deprivation.

The rise in hunger, from 20 million in 1980 to over 50 million Americans today, has risen dramatically under decades of Republican *"survival of the fittest"* Social Darwin food policies, temporary work, and subsistence wages. And with the Republican 2025 tariff war consumer goods are rising daily. Today over 50% of the population is bankrupt and many of America's impoverished communities are forced to exist with food insecurity. The Conservative ideology of the *"freedom to starve"* doesn't allow Republican non-government intervention politics to address food deprivation and child hunger that will ensure every American has enough to eat. *"Everyone has the right to starve" is basic Republican ideological doctrine."*

But, then, money is always there for trillion dollar foreign wars, trillion dollar bank bailouts, and recurring trillion dollar wealthy tax cuts, but nothing coming from Conservative legislation that will provide for the "surplus" unworthy forgotten and abandoned in the impoverished America of Republican greed.

Since at least 1964, Republicans have pushed to end Social Security though making Social Security voluntary, privatized Social Security accounts, and Social Security vouchers. The Republican political establishment has and is presently relentlessly and ruthlessly pursuing the Conservative *"every man for himself"* core agenda for the political elimination of the people's medical Affordable Care Act, Social Security, Medicare and Medicaid. Might we ask ourselves in this decisive electoral moment, what will we become of America as a free democratic people in 2026 in the face of recurring Republican wealthy tax cuts and the political demise of America's human infrastructure in a Republican "fascist" world of absolute power. The election of 2026 will decide forever what remains of America's "social safety net" the ability of everyday Americans to retirement with something, and the transfer of America's three trillion dollar Social Security Trust Fund to the private sector.

Every voter in 2026 must keep in mind, once the Republicans have legislatively abolished the affordable healthcare Social Security, Medicare and Medicaid, *"You're on your own"* as just "surplus" in a conservative American world of the *"survival of the fittest."*

LATE AFTERNOON

Your teen age daughter, Lidia, is involved in an automobile accident and rushed to the hospital. As you enter the emergency room, the attending physician walks over to you and says, "I'm sorry madam, but we were unable to treat your daughter. We've been advised that you do not have healthcare insurance coverage. I'm sure you can understand this medical facility is a "For-Profit" enterprise. Unless you are in a position to make a "cash payment" at this time, I'm afraid there's nothing we can do for your daughter. It's a miracle she made it this far. You see, she didn't 'by law' have any Authorized Private Medical ID on her person at the time of the accident. Technically, she should not have been transported to this clinic. I'm sorry, but only cash payment or private insurance coverage for medical care is the law of the land. Please call our Patient Processing Center tomorrow for final arrangements and any outstanding fee adjustments.

**FOR
DEMOCRACY
TO
LET FREEDOM RING
EVERY VOTE MATTERS**

POEM

QUIET DESPERATION

TODAY I face the uncertainty
Of a suffering people living
In "Quiet Desperation"

TODAY I endure the misery
Of "Trickle-Down"
Poverty and Despair

TODAY I struggle to survive
The betrayal of
Conservative Extremism

TODAY I know this day
May be my everyday
For all my tomorrows

BEYOND DARKNESS

FRIDAY EVENING

As the twilight fades into early darkness, Bill and Martha relax in the quiet aftermath of a very difficult and trying day. Suddenly Mary exclaims, "I'm worried! Bill! I'm Scared!" Bill, picking up on Mary's sense of alarm, is about to speak when Mary continues, "I just can't see how we're going to get through the winter. Money's very tight right now, but it's more than that Bill. There's just not enough money anymore to meet basic needs; we're barely keeping up with food, rent, and taxes. Since the Republicans abandoned Social Security and Medicare, most of what little income we bring in goes to medical expenses.

"I do appreciate how you feel" Martha, "we lost our pensions to the plant closure in the "Hedge Fund" hostile takeover debacle, and the money that came from the forced sale of the house due to rising property taxes just vanished in last year's speculation financial collapse."

After a long pause, Bill says, "You know, Martha, we're over 70 years old, worked hard all our lives to raise three children, and sacrificed to remain debt free. Yet we find ourselves struggling to survive in our last days. And we're not alone. Most of the young families in the neighborhood with only part-time low-wage work are in the same situation. However, there is some good news: the election is next month."

"Now - That - Is - Just - Great!" Martha responds with a sigh, "The Republicans have promised economic growth, more jobs, and prosperity "even for the poor" for decades, and all that's left for most of us is subsistence living, increasing debt, and tax cuts for the wealthy."

Martha, looking at Bill with some hesitation, continues, "and now with the everyday revelations of corruption, hypocrisy, and lawlessness driving Republican politics in the nation's capital, there sits a deceiver reminiscent of 1505 Rome when 'there was no outrage or crime that was not openly practiced in the Palace. The Prince was an abyss of vice, a subverter of all justice. All feared him. Men were thrown into the Tiber and despoiled of all possessions at his orders.'"

"Unless democracy triumphs over the darkness of financial greed, legal corruption, and political injustice of the moment, Bill, the alternative for future generations is the final death knell of what remains of yesterday's moral, cultural, and social values that was the bedrock of American democracy for over two hundred years."

"I know," Bill laments, "I understand all too well, Martha. We are in every sense a people politically betrayed, abandoned, and forgotten. And here we are, Martha, just *"surplus" people"* existing in a Conservative swamp of injustice, corruption, and greed"

II

The inference of "betrayal" by the Republicans and the financial power elite of which Galbraith makes reference still begs the question: How should we a People of Liberty, who swear allegiance to protect the Constitution of the United States against all "enemies" foreign and domestic, view an American "special interest" political economic takeover of America's democratic institutions and the livelihood of the American people?

The Constitution is cogently clear the "national interest" of the nation is the "general Welfare" of the people. Do we not as a nation consider any adversary as any person, nation, or ideology with an intent or action to harm the "national interest" and the American way of life? More to the point, when we ask ourselves, *"who do we say we are,"* do we consider the essence of *"who we are"* is everyone's ability to live secure and experience "the blessings of liberty" in a just and economically stable democracy? Do we see in ourselves the Founder's meaning of the "Declaration of Independence" as the embodiment every person's "inalienable right to life"? Do we feel in our everyday Conservative "Trickle- Down" world of *every man for himself"* the assurance of a functional democracy comes down to you and me, our children, and our posterity?

It is for us, a People of Liberty, to behold that this "country belongs to the people," and the right of citizenship embodies the Constitutional right to exercise *the power and the duty to protect themselves and their own welfare," and the political will to,*

> **RETURN** Constitutional preeminence to America's representational democratic governance;

> **RESTORE** the protection of the "general Welfare" as the primary imperative of the "national interest;"

> **RENEW** America's founding "life" imperative of every person's "Inalienable Right to Life," equal access to a secure living-wage, affordable healthcare and education; and "equal justice before the law";

> **ABOLISH** America's "dark money" electoral financial dominance for public funded campaign financing.

Clearly every suffering American living poor in desperation and despair understands the political reality of today's "big money" dominated predatory culture of *"Profit over People"* is not the democratic America of Washington, Jefferson, and Lincoln. The political and economic "financial bondage" of the Conservative *Lives for Profit Subsistence Trickle-Down Society* is nothing less than the return of the "let them eat cake" culture of divine right governance. The Republican brutal everyday culture of mercantile greed now dominates the life of every citizen and impoverished family struggling to survive the tragic human suffering, misery, and despair of the Republican "Trickle-Down" economic agenda. It now falls to the people as Lord Acton reminds us, "... *to make up for the want of legal responsibility ... for absolute power corrupts absolutely."*

Today the **"CALL OF LIBERTY"** beckons a free democratic People, conceived in "Liberty, Equality, and Justice," **to a Great Patriotic Renewa**l of Integrity, Trust, and Truth to a Democratic America politically free of "dark money" political-economic dominance and **a Rebirth of American Democracy** that restores,

> **"We the People" are a Representative Democratic Republic "Of the People" dedicated to the rule of law, equal opportunity, and the Constitutional rights of citizenship to "Life, Liberty, and the "Pursuit of Happiness" for "Ourselves and Our Posterity."**

The political-economic suffering of today's Republican predatory *"survival of the fittest"* culture of individual extremism and concentrated wealth brings to mind echoes of yesterday's freedom that cries out for a People of Liberty united in Freedom to VOTE in 2026 for the return to an American democracy "Of, By, and For" the people. Some points to consider in the restoration of a people's Constitutional Democratic America of "Freedom, Equality, and Justice for All" would include the following:

ABOLISH "Corporate Personhood;

CONTROL GLOBAL WARMING through a measured public policy to transform America's fossil fuel dependency to a 21st Century American Renewable Clean Energy Infrastructure;

DECREE a mandated living-wage income, affordable national healthcare and education, a government insured portable pension retirement plan, and consumer product safety protection;

DEMILITARIZE the law enforcement culture of punitive extremism;

END private "Prisons for Profit" and all outsourced privatized government services;

ENFORCE the Sherman Antitrust Act and regulatory control over acquisitions and mergers;

ENSURE everyone contributes a fair share to the national income, citizens, non-citizen residents, and all forms business profitability;

IMPOSE regulatory controls and tax liability on Hedge Fund and Private Equity operations;

LEGISLATE binding procedural mandates and real-time oversight accountability measures regardless of the political party in power that will ensure the unrestricted function of America's Constitutional three co-equal branches of government;

LEVY a transaction tax on monetary instruments bought and sold;

MANDATE American ownership of domestic media networks that impact the national interest and truth oversight accountability;

MODERENIZE the national infrastructure with a comprehensive public funded National Infrastructure Public Works Program;

PROHIBIT "dark money" campaign financing, voter suppression, and political district gerrymandering;

REAFFIRM America's "inalienable to the right to life" as a right of citizenship for all generations to come;

REFORM America's electoral political process through legislation to (1) guarantee the voting rights of every American citizen, (2) provide public funded campaign financing, and (3) abolish the Electoral College;

REINSTATE deregulated controls and protections for the oversight accountability commercial investment institutions;

RESTORE parliamentary principles of legislative procedure that enforce a fair representation of the people's "general welfare" and will of the electorate;

RETURN to the economic principles of a well regulated competitive fair market economy;

REVIVE the "rule of law," equal justice under the law, and oversight accountability for American finance, business, and politics;

STRENGTHEN America's democratic institutions, breakup "too-big- to-fail" monopolies that include big tech giants, broad-casting and media consortiums, and financial institutions and cartels.

III

As citizens of freedom and democracy struggling to endure the "Trickle-Down" reality of want, desperation, and despair in this *"survival of the fittest"* Republican moment, Supreme Court Justice Louis D. Brandeis warned that we must as a People of Liberty be informed and vigilant to the greed, perils, and injustice of wealth concentration in the hands of a few, emphasizing that ,

> *"We may have democracy*
> *or we may have*
> *concentrated wealth*
> *in the hands of a few,*
> *but we can't have both."*

The concentration and control of America's wealth *"in the hands of a few"* politically assured by an entrenched Republican

123

power base are the defining focus of the Conservative "Trickle-Down" predatory *"survival of the fittest"* political agenda. For no other reason this is the economic predatory objective of the "dark money" political takeover of America and its institutions, and the inability of America's workers to secure productive living wage employment.

The Founding mechanism of Constitutional "checks and balances" of co-equal branches of government was designed specifically to prevent the exercise of authoritarian power and the concentration of wealth in the hands of a privileged plutocacy. The Forty-Year Republican takeover of America's political and economic institutions is for every suffering American today the struggle to survive the Conservative political-economic oppression of the Republican predatory "Trickle-Down" subsistence economy. The question before us fundamental to the future of American democracy in an America of "Liberty and Justice for All" is uncomplicated and straightforward: Are we a People of Liberty willing to electorally confront America's Republican ideological *"survivalist"* political reality of fascist greed, poverty, and desperation?

Yesterday's free democratic America is today's free democratic people infused as in days gone by with Liberty's most cherished values of Freedom. Is it for us, the electorate of America, to redress the American tragedy of Conservative predatory "Trickle-Down" poverty and desperation, and return America to a Constitutional democracy of living-wage jobs, universal lifesaving healthcare, affordable education and housing, and for all Americans a long hard-earned dignified retirement.

For decades the Republican political dominance over America's democracy and its political institutions has abrogated the Constitutional obligations of the state to the Conservative "dark money" power establishment of *"individual" freedom* *"without a network of obligations"* to pillage and plunder at will whatever the collateral damage.

In societies historically akin to an ideological "Social Darwin" political economy in times past, history suggests that citizenship in such a political order of "individual extremism" is inevitably tied to political reliability and restraint. And, the politically designated "unworthy" who consume the valuable resources of the state will be subject to some form of state sanction. Is this the coming final "Trickle-Down" ideological reality of the new age of American "individual extremism?" Is this advanced Conservative Social Darwin Society to be a *"survival of the world"* of Euthanasia Care Centers for the terminally ill and Forced Labor Camps for the "unworthy surplus people" of America struggling day-to-day to survive as political "vermin," freeloaders" and "parasites," the vulnerable, the destitute, the disabled, the elderly retired living in poverty?

Is this not the time for every citizen to examine how we see ourselves as a Constitutional people whose Founder Fathers endeavored to guarantee that the *"nation exists to serve its citizens"* and the function of responsible government is to promote and protect the "general Welfare" of the people?

Yesterday's competitive free market capitalism based on supply and demand died in the 1980 election of the Republican

"Supply Side" Revolution and the subsequent Republican legislated predatory *"Profit over People"* subsistence debt-based casino America. Today's America of income inequality, poverty, hunger, and homelessness is the realization of the Republican legislated transformation of an American democracy that once embraced the security and the welfare of the "American family" as the cornerstone imperative of the nation.

In a democracy "OF, BY, and FOR" the People, it is the function of government to provide the means necessary for every citizen to be able to earn a respectable living-wage and live a dignified quality of life in economic security, peace, and justice. The resolution to today's *"crisis in democracy"* is nothing less than a return to a prosperous America for the many NOT the few. It is for us, the people of America, to protect "the general Welfare" in a democratic America "of the people" that will deliver to America's People of Liberty the civil liberties, economic security, and Justice under the law through:

IV

I often wonder in these difficult times how a democratic people relate to the reality of truth in a corrupt predatory world of "alternative facts". Truth, of course, is what it always has been, the reality of what is supported by personal observation or reliable documented facts. I still see the "Truth" in this political era of Republican autocracy that confuses a democratic people through political lies, deceit, and subterfuge that seek to hide the reality of what is hidden in the shadows of greed, corruption, and injustice.

I see that America once prosperous, stable, and secure, an America at economic peace when the reality of the America Dream was limited only to one's desire, will, and courage to make it happen. I see a time when America was the Beacon of Liberty, when everyone had access to a productive living-wage job, affordable healthcare, housing, and education, and the promise of a retirement with dignity in old age. I see an America that was for a People of Liberty the Golden Age of the American experience, a time we celebrated as a free democratic people a shared belief in an America of *"one Nation under God."*

The America of personal liberty and income prosperity that once was but a generation ago is gone - dead, dismantled and discarded – stolen from a trusting democratic People of Liberty through decades of political betrayal in the name of fairy-tale profits, wealth concentration, and the elimination of middle class America that today has left the American people shattered and impoverished in a Republican predatory "Trickle-Down" Subsistence Society.

Conservative "Trickle-Down" prosperity was sold in 1980 as the Republican life- saving program that would resolve the economic downturn of the 1970s, create higher paying jobs, and extend prosperity to everyone. The political reality, of course, is that the Republican political establishment transformed America over four decades of political deception and deceit into a nation of polarization, political manipulation and disinformation, and an America of *"surplus"* people *"responsible for their own fate."*

The consequences of this four-decade Republican "fascist" campaign of political oppression is that we are a disenfranchised democratic people who daily bear witness to ugly Republican legislative autocratic governance, institutional paralysis, political corruption, and the overt political emasculation of justice. This is the *"you're on your own"* Conservative "fascist" world of Republican legislated *"individual extremism"* of the *"survival of the fittest."* At its crux, it is a Conservative orchestrated political-economic world where people struggle daily to make ends meet with a subsistence existence of little work, poverty wages, and a lifetime of chronic debt.

V

We see across the nation an America politically and economically bankrupt America on the verge of economic collapse at any given moment for the sole benefit of enriching the financial power elite. And, tragically, only a few are given to acknowledge the real elephant in the room for what it is: the "dark money" predatory ideological world of "political economy" in the name of business efficiency, maximum profitability, and monopoly dominance that mandates the people of America are *"responsible for their own fate,"* every citizen has the freedom to "fend for himself," to *"become surplus,"* and exercise the *"freedom to starve"* in a Conservative financialized subsistence-wage debt-based predatory economy.

The American Citizen in today's Republican predatory world is a non-person, just a disposable pawn, mercantile fodder in a Conservative world of wealth creation oblivious to the suffering of the America people and the Constitutional mandate to protect the welfare of the people.

Keep in mind the lost jobs, national hunger, and human desperation that is the core of the Conservative political reality of the Social Darwin "political economy" is upfront in proclaiming "the more surplus workers, the more profitable our operations." And for everybody else, well, it's just the same old Conservative predatory reality of your everyday *survival of the fittest* America of organized systemic exploitation, struggle, and desperation.

The Founding Fathers would be appalled to witness the moral transformation and political descent of America into what today is a Republican predatory impoverished America of national greed and corruption, concentrated wealth, and political hypocrisy.

The truth hurts, we are told. Of course, the truth hurts. And the truth for today's America of Washington, Jefferson, and Madison is there's nothing more "liberating" than the feeling of "Freedom, Equality, and Justice" that can relieve the pain of injustice. For today's Republican subsistence America the pain of injustice can only be remedied with a return to pure democracy, productive living-wage jobs, affordable lifesaving healthcare for all, and retirement security in an America "Liberty and Justice for All."

We are what we believe and the values we hold most sacred: freedom, family, truth, fairness, justice, concern for another's well being. We each have the "liberty" to do that which is good, just, and honest. It is these values "We the People" have asserted over the generations to one and all of what it means to be a citizen of America. To believe in an America of "Liberty, Equality, and Justice" is for every patriotic American to proclaim and honor through the democratic process the values that assure "Liberty and Justice for All".

Surely, "PATRIOTISM" is loyalty first to the Constitution. America's founding values of Truth, Freedom, Democracy, and the Rule of Law" define who we are as a democratic People of Liberty.

Now, as we debate our children's political world of tomorrow in 2026, the political imperative for each of us is to keep upper most in our political consciousness the reality of who are, a patriotic people of Liberty, Truth, and Justice.

FOR
DEMOCRACY
TO
LET FREEDOM RING
EVERY VOTE MATTERS

POEM

FREEDOM LOST

To Be DOWNTRODDEN
Subjugated and Exploited
IS NOT FREEDOM!

To Be IMPOVERISHED
Desperate and Hopeless
IS NOT FREEDOM!

To Be MARGINALIZED
Rejected and Scorned
IS NOT FREEDOM!

To Be SURPLUS
Abandoned and Alone
IS NOT FREEDOM!

FREEDOM OR FASCISM

VICE PRESIDENT
Henry Wallace

ON
AMERICAN FASCISM

The method of American fascism "is to poison the channels of public information.

With the fascist the problem is never how best to present the truth to the public but how best to use the news to deceive the public into giving the fascist and his group more money or more power.

The American fascist claims *"to be super patriots, but they would destroy every liberty guaranteed by the constitution.*

The American fascist "demands free enterprise but they are spokesmen for monopoly and vested interests.

The American fascist's "final objective is directed to the capture of political power so that, using the power of the state and the power of the market simultaneously, they may keep the common man in eternal subjugation."

The triumph of the Republican 40-year campaign to rescue "capitalism from democracy," financially subjugate the people of America, and lay the foundation for the political takeover of democracy is today the Conservative "Social Darwin" reality of a suffering democratic people. In a generation, the body politic of America has been *"turned upside down"* into a Republican ideological state of the *"survival of the fittest,"* a predatory deregulated debt-based America of concentrated wealth in the hands of a few, "dark money" used to attack the very foundational notion of government "by and for" the people. January 6, 2021, make no mistake, was America's "Rubicon" moment. For every American in today's electoral moment *"the die is cast."* **Today in 2026, we vote as a People of Liberty for the political future of America, be it *DEMOCRACY OR AUTOCRACY* for all of our tomorrows.**

The strength of who we are as a People of Liberty *"is seen in the things we stand for,"* Theodore Roosevelt reminds us. While the political-economic reality of America before us since the advent of the 1981 Republican "Trickle-Down" Revolution is but a Conservative predatory *"survival of the fittest"* world of vulture capitalism, lawless exploitation, and suppression of basic civil liberties. The things we stand for as a People of Liberty have not changed: Constitutional Democracy, the rule of law, secure living-wage jobs, and the "inalienable right to life, and the pursuit of happiness." This is the idea of America; this is our founding birthright; this is who we are as a People of Liberty. The hold of political "individual extremism" manifested in today's Republican ideological world of the *"survival of the fittest"* is the reality of the Conservative Culture of Death shrouded in a web of lies that blind, deafen, and deceive.

The destructive "evil" of "designing men" of wealth and power reigns over the political Betrayal of America in this electoral moment. The reality of authoritarian despotism has to date permitted the Republican ideology of political "extremism" to tear down the ability of the American people to purse the blessings of "life, liberty, and pursuit of happiness."

As a People of Liberty in 2026, remember,

> The **REPUBLICAN** financialized debt-based subsistence-wage, casino economy;

> The **REPUBLICAN** state racially oriented voter rights suppression laws disenfranchising tens of millions of voters;

> The **REPUBLICAN** state voter nullification laws overruling the "will of the people;"

The **REPUBLICAN** "rigged" gerrymandering of state voter districts in pursuit of Conservative "white power" supremacy;

The **REPUBLICAN** state pandemic anti-vaccine political initiatives that unnecessarily has caused over a million Covid deaths;

The **REPUBLICAN** "Climate Change Denial" legislative obstruction in the name of "Profit over People" destroying our children's world of tomorrow;

The **REPUBLICAN** legislative "obstruction" politics blocking America's "democratic" human infrastructure for lifting working families out of poverty and the human bondage of profit supremacy.

The Conservative Fifty-Year grand strategy for a protracted Republican transformation of American democracy is now the Republican "Project 2025" for,

DISMANTLING America's political and state institutions;

POLITIZING the government career "civil service;"

DEREGULATION of the "rule of law" into a politically acceptable state of "lawlessness" in politics, business, finance, and government;

TAX CUTS in the trillions of dollars for the ultra-rich and corporations;

PRIVATIZATION of Social Security, Medicare, and the medical Affordable Care Act; and, most importantly,

POLITICAL SUBVERSION of democratic norms, intensifying ethnic and cultural division, and inciting violence to radicalize supporters to divide the body politic;

DISINFORMATION poisoning of the public discourse;

SEIZURE of absolute power by any means at whatever the cost.

ELIMINATION of wealthy and corporate taxation; and

MARGINALIZATION of the elderly, the disabled, the poor and homeless in a Conservative world where *"everyone has the right to starve"* in a Republican America committed to the *"survival of the fittest."*

The Republican campaign agenda for 2026 is the political promise to literally restructure American Democracy into a 1930s racist authoritarian model of "fascism."

Four decades of Republican political economic and social engineering for the concentration of wealth and power of America presents the electorate with a compromised America on the fringe of forever losing the cherished freedoms of democracy, and a Constitutional America dedicated to the "rule of law," equal opportunity, and the common good. *"The spirit of resistance to government is so valuable on certain occasions,"* **wrote Thomas Jefferson** in a letter to Abigail Adams in 1787, *"I wish it always to be kept alive."* That "certain occasion" for today's besieged democratic America is so blatantly and visibly present in the perverse human suffering that pervades the people of America.

America's 2026 electoral moment is America's electoral grand finale of the **Conservative 40-year REPUBLICAN ASSAULT ON DEMOCRACY** and political Betrayal of the American People. The Conservative political reality of want, desperation, and despair and the concentration of America's wealth and power in the hands of "designing men" is in this moment the Republican Conservative "Project 2025," the *Republican political promise of "nationcide" for America, meaning the present dismantling of American democracy as in "the extermination of the national civilization a people have built – customs, traditions, civil associations and practices of self-government."* Consider we must as a People of Liberty the future of America as we reflect on where we stand as a suffering democratic people of "liberty" after 40 years of Republican political betrayal:

> **First, reflect on the present reality of President Franklin Roosevelt's warning that "fascism" would come to America in the form of profit supremacy and monopoly dominance, if *"the people tolerate the growth of private power ... Democracy is not safe if its business system does not provide employment ...***

in such a way as to sustain an acceptable standard of living" for its people.

Second, consider that following the 1971 Powell declaration of "war against democracy" and the people of America, **the Republican political establishment set out to reconstruct America,** the criminal justice system, and the electoral system in favor of the wealthy power elite. **Through deregulation, privatization, wealthy tax cuts, and voter restrictions, American democracy is today a nation of wealth and power concentrated in the 1%, a "financialized" world of profiteers, and an economy of monopolized production and distribution. For "We the People,"** the everyday reality is the subsistence debt-based existence of service jobs, poverty-wages, and, for many, an impoverished retirement on the streets of America.

Third, understand that American democracy today is the hands of the Conservative financial power who have relentlessly sought to marginalize democracy, morality, and truth, to usurp the power of the state, and through the power of "dark money" reconfigure America's Republican state legislatures to ensure forever a Conservative hold on political power. Today we must bear in mind the waning of **Dietrich Bonheoffer: "TO SEE EVIL AND NOT CALL IT EVIL IS EVIL; NOT TO SPEAK IS TO SPEAK; NOT TO ACT IS TO ACT."**

The political-economic reality of America is everywhere evident across a suffering America where the Conservative ideological extremism of unhampered capital supremacy of the *"survival of the fittest"* reigns supreme over the lives of an abandoned "surplus" people and the demise of American democracy.

With the Republican obstruction of the National Voting Rights Act, the Republican political establishment laid the groundwork to achieve the "fascist" authoritarianism of absolute power supremacy. America's democratic heritage, traditions, and institutions have been successfully eroded for the Conservative elimination of democracy itself in America. **Given Republican control of Congress in 2026, the Republican political *"assault on democracy"* envisioned in the "Powell Memorandum" of 1971 to save "capitalism from democracy" will forever hold America's free democratic people in the human bondage of want, desperation, and despair."**

Across America, from the Atlantic to the Pacific, from the mountains and prairies to the desert wastelands, in the cities, and in the towns and villages, America's great democracy is under siege. **Notes former Republican Max Boot,** author of *The Corrosion of Conservatism: Why I Left the Right (2018),* **"I have no faith that we will remain a democracy if Republicans win power."** The political reality in 2026 is America's democratic "survival" moment that will determine forever whether the promise of Freedom, Equality, and Justice in America is to survive into a "new age" of Constitutional governance "for the people" of America

In 2020, the people of America voted to renew **Martin Luther King's dream** of an "equal" America, an America that values the "inalienable right to life" over wealth creation, an America whose birthright of "liberty and justice for all" **calls each of us to undo the burden of political "dark money" tyranny, break the bonds of greed, corruption, and injustice, and ensure a decent standard of living for every American.**

The *"spirit of resistance"* **called for by Thomas Jefferson in times of tyrannical national peril demands "We the People" in 2026 come together to "constitutionally" resolve the Republican corruption of democracy in this American moment.**

The Election of 2026 is the "last battle" in the coming final struggle for DEMOCRACY in America. For the people of America in this apocalyptic electoral moment, **Edmund Burke warned in the 18th Century,** *"THE ONLY THING FOR EVIL TO TRIUMPH IS FOR GOOD PEOPLE TO DO NOTHING."*

"You cannot escape the responsibility of tomorrow," warned Abraham Lincoln, *"by evading it today."* Tomorrow's political reality of Freedom and Democracy in America is in our hands "of the people." **The choice for every citizen in 2026 as historian Matt Stoller remarked in 2019:** *"we vote to knowingly allow a small aristocracy governing ... to serve concentrated power, or free ourselves from concentrated power."*

The Hour has Come; the Moment is Here; the time is Now for the return of Democracy, Truth, and Justice to an America "Of the People, By the People, For the People."

2026 may very well be America's "one time" opportunity for a free democratic people to EMBRACE the reality of an America "In God We Trust;" RETURN the "rule of law" to business, finance, and politics; and RESTORE *America's founding vision of government that will "insure domestic Tranquility … establish Justice … promote the general Welfare … and secure the Blessings of Liberty … for ourselves and our posterity."*

FOR
DEMOCRACY
TO
LET FREEDOM RING
EVERY VOTE MATTERS

POEM

AWAKE AMERICA

There stands
our once
Great Democracy
Today
Betrayed and Abandoned
Destitute In the Shambles
Of Want and Despair
Gone
Our Livelihood
Stability and Security
Our Cherished Freedoms
Now
Just Rampant Corruption
"Trickle-Down" Servitude
And Desperation for All

THE 1984 REALITY

Suspended amid the corruption
Of state sponsored desperation I ask
myself "Who Am I" in this political
Sea of iniquity and deceit?

I see across the landscape of freedom
Skies of darkness awash in the pain
Of a suffering people longing for
Liberty, Truth, and Justice

I know in my anguish and sorrow,
I am but a "surplus" unworthy
Existing between hope and despair
in a politically betrayed America

I feel in my trepidation I am
The "surplus" fodder of empty
Political promises struggling in a
Lives for Profit political economy

I strive with each new passing day to
Survive the plunder and exploitation of
A nation gasping for life in a rich
wasteland of political greed and injustice

**Now as I face the sham and treachery
Of today's autocratic reality I live
For the return of an America of
Liberty and Justice for All**

When we hear talk of autocracy, authoritarianism, or dictatorship, for most of us the name Orwell comes to mind. In his futuristic novel "1984," Orwell gives an illustration of what life would be without freedom. Only "Big Brother" is permitted to think, reason, and decide. When people are converted to believe in "Big Brother," slavery is born! The warning here is 'the "1984" reality' can happen anywhere if people do not become aware of the political assault on their personal freedom.

The term "Trickle-Down Prosperity" lays bare the privatized "political economy" of human bondage in today's Conservative *"every man for himself"* America of a democratic peoples' lost political freedom.

The Social Darwin "political economy" of "Trickle-Down" poverty is the political-economic narrative of today's America. When the financial barons and mercantile monopolies realized they had no other worlds to conquer, the financiers, profiteers and speculators in their quest for quick profits, plundered the national wealth, worker's wages, and the personal assets of their own people.

When the politically engineered thievery and abject poverty of America came home to roost as in 1929 and 2008, America's financial "house of cards" came crashing down. As a consequence of the financial growth gimmicks, market manipulation, trader speculation, corporate raiders, and private equity plundering of

America's infrastructure, the financial bubbles burst, the markets collapsed, and massive widespread financial disaster resulted in bank runs, depression, and massive unemployment.

The "political-economic" dynamic in each era of greed, corruption, and injustice follows a familiar pattern: early growth and wealth accumulation, financial entitlements, accrual of investment "hot" money from wealthy tax cuts and deregulation, mega-mergers, monopolistic control of the economy, transfer of middle class wealth to the Ultra-Rich, and massive unrestrained "speculation" followed by an unsound economy and economic collapse.

Millions of Americans become unemployed, homeless, and hungry. In the final draw, with the massed wealth of the private investment schemes, financial roulette, and political maneuvers of the "big money" power brokers, the wealth of the nation is concentrated in the hands of the 1% protected by government legislated taxpayer bailouts, all at the expense of the political betrayal of a "surplus" people abandoned, forgotten, and *"left to their own fate."*

II

"The decision to include or exclude those lying wounded along the roadside can serve as a criterion for judging every economic, political, and social project. Each day we have to decide whether to be Good Samaritans or indifferent bystanders."
"Fratelli Tutti"

145

Conservative political ideology advocates subscribe to the political-economic folly of "non-governmental interference" in the economy, non-governmental interference in reducing poverty, and non-governmental interference in providing for the people's "common good," be it healthcare, hunger, or any other human need.

Historian Bruce Ingalls recounts in The Opium War, the "political economy" of **Mill, Ricardo, and McCulloch** in the 19th Century was used to foster the justification workers *"had no right to more than a bare living for themselves and their families."* To the argument at the time this was unjust, Ingles notes the political economists were given to respond: *"the alternative for many families might be starvation ... this form of culling was necessary ... to prevent over population where resources were limited.*

In The Surplus American, Derber and Magrass examine the fundamentals of the ideological basis of "political economy." The political philosophy of the Republican Conservative "big money" political establishment in today's "Pooring of America" is the Social Darwin Doctrine of the *"survivalist of the fittest."* It is the fundamental cause the people of America must endure such hardship in this political moment. Why we ask?

> **First, For the Conservative,** *"Everyone [is] entitled to an equal opportunity to prove their merit on the market. Those who fail deserve their fate" "Nobody owes you nothin." Democracy offers individual freedom ... that is "Freedom from a network of obligations, Freedom to fend for yourself; but also Freedom to become "surplus," and Freedom to starve." People are responsible for their own fate."*

Second, the crux of today's desperation and despair across America, is the Conservative political Social Darwin imperative: *"suffering, even deaths, among the poor [are] part of a natural winnowing process necessary to separate the worthy from the unworthy ... [the] misery and mortality or the unworthy [are] a necessary cost for creating unprecedented prosperity; [and] the "surplus" people, "the starving the homeless, the vagabond," the freeloaders" and "parasites, just ship them off to forced labor surplus people detention centers."*

In keeping with the early proponents of "political economy," the Republican Conservative political establishment is today a "wholly owned subsidiary" of "big money" vested interests committed to maximum short-term profitability at whatever the cost to the American people. Through the political cleansing of yesterday's America of secure, productive economy of industrial strength, and the gradual dismantling of America's infrastructure to the predatory Conservative *"every man for himself"* "political economy," the reality for America's People of Liberty, once prosperous and secure, is today a bankrupt, debt-ridden, subsistence casino America of declining work, subsistence-wages, and an ever increasing cost of living of want, desperation, and despair.

America's *"survival of the fittest"* "political economy" today is the fulfillment of the Republican decades-long Social Darwin reality of financial deregulation, market manipulation, and political polarization in the drive to dismantle America's democratic institutions and secure the political dominance to restructure America into an autocratic state of the financial power elite. However politically disguised, America's Social

Darwin "political economy" is the Republican cornerstone of today's political reality of *"you're on you own"* ideological purity of *"every man for himself."*

WEDNESDAY AFTERNOON

BREAKING NEWS: ABE News has just learned that the government is about to deploy federal troops to America's "democratic" cities to contain and attack the "enemy within.

Martha, listening to the news, looks over at Bill, and asks, "Well, what do make of that, Bill?

"Not a surprise, Martha. This is the coming reality of the Republican "Project 2025" political offensive to consolidate absolute power and subjugate the people of America. Think about it. So far in less than a year, we've seen day one" dictatorship; the dismantling of America's democratic order and institutions; rollback of basic "civil rights: the suppression of free speech and the political assault on the media, the judiciary, and science; "executive" cancellation of "birth right" citizenship; removal of career non-political "civil servants" in mass; rising food prices now beyond the ability of the American people to meet basic needs; legislation giving the Ultra-Rich and corporations trillion dollar tax cuts while cutting billions from affordable healthcare and food assistance; state "prosecution" of political enemies; people seized from the streets of America without warrant or due process; and now the deployment of federal troops to "democratic cities." What's next? Well, Martha, believe me, we've seen nothing yet."

"Yes, I understand, Bill. America is in every sector of American life a Republican political-economic autocracy of monopoly supremacy, subsistence-wages, financial growth gimmicks, speculation schemes, and the destructive hedge fund pillaging of America."

But it's more than that, Martha. "There's no question we are a *"surplus people left behind"* a people struggling to secure the basic necessities of life. Now we must all come to terms with the "Project 2025" reality of the Social Darwin "political economy": NO more Social Security, Medicare, and Medicaid; NO more affordable Healthcare; NO more nutrition programs. And NO more government involvement in the lives of the American people." I'm afraid the Conservative goal here is to cull the population of America of all who it considers to be the "surplus unworthy" in the new political order: be it the marginalized, the elderly, the disabled, the poor, the homeless, and, to be sure, the politically designated "vermin" and "rabble" of the "fascist" state."

"You know, Bill, when I see the political reality of the Republican drive to restructure America into a "fascist" police state of concentrated wealth, I have trouble trying to understand how this could happen in an America founded on the "common good," the people's "inalienable right to life," and "the blessings of liberty." Didn't 85% of the people of America not so long ago declare themselves to be Christian?"

"Given the majority presence of Christians in today's America, I find it detestable, Bill, that with all the talk of Conservative Christian values, the Republican religious right subscribe to the Republican political mantra of *"every man for himself"* absent any Government involvement in the lives of the people. Surely they must know that Christian teaching *"emphasizes the equal dignity and value of every human person. That Christian tradition instructs [the faithful] to put the needs of the poor and vulnerable first. The moral status of a society is determined at a basic level by how its poorest and most vulnerable members are fairing. And so ... the preferential option for the poor is a concern not only for us individuals, but for us as a society.* For every Christian comes the call to provide for the *"marginalized, the poor and powerless [and] to love one's neighbor [as one's self]."* The reality of America's Freedom, Bill, is what the Founders made clear for a nation *"In God We Trust,"*: *"we are all really responsible for all."*

"Each day, Bill, I am often reminded of the warning Henry Wallace gave to the people of America on American Fascism: *"with the fascist the problem is never how best to present the truth to the public but how best to use the news to deceive the public ... "* The Republican political reality today is what President Franklin Roosevelt remarked during the Great Depression: *"when a Republican's lips are moving – he's lying."* It's not that surprising, Bill, the Christian right bought into the Conservative Social Darwin ideology of the *"survival of the fittest."*

"I hear you, Martha, a nation's decision to exclude from society the marginalized, the sick and the poor is a political act reminiscent of the 1930s. In a "fascist" world of capital supremacy and political corruption, we see what the Psalms record: *"the common people are as worthless as a puff of wind, and the powerful are not what they appear to be,"* [but *in time], "their own tongues will ruin them, and all who see them will shake their heads in scorn."*

"Now, Martha, it is for the people of America to restore the nation's Constitutional "checks and balances" for a rebirth of American freedom. If not, the Republicans are hell bent on achieving their decades long goal of achieving the Social Darwin "political economy" for America. It all depends on every citizen doing their patriotic duty. The future of Democracy and Freedom in America is at stake. Every ballot cast in 2026 is a ballot about one issue, and one issue only: *THE POWER TO PRESERVE OR DESTROY DEMOCRACY IN AMERICA."*

The election of 2026, Martha, will determine who we say we are as a People of Liberty. My hope is we will choose wisely through the strength of moral conviction for an America *"IN GOD WE TRUST."* Should the people of America choose unwisely, I'm afraid the future for America's People of Liberty will be *"The '1984' Reality" of the "Peoples' Coming Apocalypse"* – and, yes, Martha, it will be for many generations to come."

"The political imperative of 2026, Martha, is for every voting American to comprehend the consequences of what Jean-Jacques Rousseau warned in a similar time: *"Free people, remember, we may acquire liberty, but it is never recovered if it is lost."*

FOR

DEMOCRACY

TO

LET FREEDOM RING

EVERY VOTE MATTERS

POEM

FREEDOM CALLING

I HEAR
The toll of
LIBERTY'S BELL
Ringing a great
PATRIOTIC RENEWAL

I HEAR the sound
Of distant drums
Echoing Freedom's Call
For LIBERTY, TRUTH,
AND JUSTICE

I HEAR above
The din of battle for
The Soul of America
Cry out for a
FREE AMERICA

I HEAR the
Sound of Liberty
Beckoning a proud
Democratic people to the
LIGHT OF A NEW DAWN

ON
AMERICAN
DEMOCRACY

With
THEODORE ROOSEVELT

*"The people have the right, the power,
and the duty to protect themselves
and their own welfare."*

"I believe in pure democracy. With Lincoln, I hold this country, with its institutions, belongs to the people who inhabit it. Whenever they shall grow weary of the existing government, they can exercise their Constitutional right of amending it."

"We Progressives believe that the people have the right, the power, and the duty to protect themselves and their own welfare; that human rights are supreme over all other rights; that wealth should be the servant, not the master, of the people."

"We believe that unless representative government does absolutely represent the people it is not representative government at all. We test the worth of all men and all

measures by asking how they contribute to the welfare of the men, women, and children of whom this nation is composed."

"We are engaged in one of the great battles of the age long contest waged against privilege on behalf of the common welfare. We hold it a prime duty of the people to free our government from the control of money in politics. For this purpose we advocate, not as ends of themselves but as weapons in the hands of the people, all government devices which will make the representatives of the people more easily and certainly responsible to the will of the people."

"This country, as Lincoln said, belongs to the people. So do the natural resources which make it rich. They supply the basis of our prosperity now and hereafter. In preserving them, which is a national duty, we must not forget that monopoly is based on the control of national resources ... and that it will help the people little to conserve our natural wealth of concentrated power and the benefits which it can yield are secured to the people. Let us remember, also ... that the principle of making the best of all have requires with equal or greater insistence that we shall stop the waste of human life in industry, and prevent the waste of human welfare which flows from the unfair use of concentrated power and wealth in the hands of men whose eagerness for profit blinds them to the cost of what they do."

"I am emphatically a believer in constitutionalism, and because of this fact I know less emphatically protest against any theory that would make the constitution a means of thwarting instead of securing the absolute right of the people

to rule themselves and to provide for their own social and industrial well-being. All constitutions – those of the states no less than that of the nation – are designed and must be interpreted and administered so as to fit human rights."

"We should discriminate between two purposes we have in view. The first is the effort to provide what are themselves the ends of good government; the second is the effort to provide proper machinery for the advancement of these ends. The ends of good government in our democracy are to secure by genuine popular rule a high average of moral and material well-being among our citizens ... The only prosperity worth having is that which affects the mass of the people ... I hold it our duty to see that the wage worker, the small producer, the ordinary consumer, shall get their fair share of the benefit of business prosperity. "Now ... It is imperative to exercise over big business ... control and supervision ... All business must be conducted under the law, and all business men, big or small, must act justly. But a wicked big interest is necessarily more dangerous to the community than a wicked little interest. Big business in the past has been responsible for much of the special privilege which must be sparingly cut out of our national life."

"Government regulation of big business is ... needed ... Among the states that have entered this field Wisconsin has taken a leading place ... They have initiated the kind of progressive government which means not merely the preservation of true democracy but the extension of the principle of true democracy into industrialism as well as politics."

"This is precisely the attitude we should take towards big business. It is the practical application of the principle of the square deal ... In other words, our demand is that big business give the people a square deal and the people give a square deal to any man engaged in big business who honestly endeavors to do what is right and proper. All business into which the element of monopoly in any way or degree ... should be carefully supervised, regulated, and controlled by government authority...[if not] broken up."

"But we should not fear, if necessary, to bring the regulation of big [business] to the point of controlling conditions so that the wage worker shall have a wage more than sufficient to cover the bare cost of living, and hours of work not so excessive as to wreck his strength by the strain of unending toil and leave him unfit to do his duty as a good citizen on the community."

"Whatever the practices upon the past of large combinations may threaten to discourage such a man or to deny to him that which in the judgment of the community is a square deal should be specifically defined by the statutes as crimes. And in every case the individual ... responsible for such unfair dealing should be punished."

"But we should so shape conditions that a fortune shall be obtained only in honorable fashion, in such fashion ... We stand for the rights of property, but we stand even more for the rights of man. We will protect the rights of the wealthy man, but we maintain that he holds his wealth subject to the

community to regulate its business use as the public welfare requires. "

Theodore Roosevelt
Exposition of American democracy
Ohio State Constitutional Convention 1912

FOR
DEMOCRACY
TO
LET FREEDOM RING
EVERY VOTE MATTERS

POEM
EVERY VOTE MATTERS

FOR
FREEDOM AND DEMOCRACY
EVERY VOTE MATTERS!

FOR
LIVING WAGE JOBS
EVERY VOTE MATTERS!

FOR
LIFE SAVING HEALTHCARE
EVERY VOTE MATTERS!

FOR
JUSTICE BEFORE THE LAW
EVERY VOTE MATTERS!

FOR
LIBERTY, TRUTH, JUSTICE
EVERY VOTE MATTERS!

FOR DEMOCRACY TO
LET FREEDOM RING
EVERY VOTE MATTERS!

TRUTH MATTERS

HISTORY IS TRUTH

"Facts are stubborn things.
Facts are true things.
Facts are reliable.
They cannot be ignored.
History is truth teaching by
example. We may miss the
truth by perverting the history,
but truth is in the facts of history."

E.M. Bounds

LET FREEDOM RING
A REFERENCE GUIDE

ANDERSEN, Kurt, *Evil Geniuses: The Unmaking of America: A Recent History* (NY: Random House, 2020)

APPLEBAUM, Anne, *Twilight of Democracy:Deliberate Dysfunction and the Battle to Preserve Democracy* (Denver: Dream Books Company, 2023)

APPLEBAUM, Anne*, Autocracy, Inc.: The Dictators Who Want to Rule the World* (NY: Doubleday, 2024).

ARNADE, Chris, Dignity: *Seeking Respect in Back Row America* (NY: Penguin Random House, 2019)

ABRAMSKY, Sasha, *The America Way of Poverty: How the Other Half Still Lives* (NY: Nation Books, 2013)

BATTISTONE, Alyssa, **"Everything to Lose: The Struggle To Save the Planet,"** The Nation,June 3/10, 2019

BARTLETT, Donald L. and James B.
STEELE, *The Betrayal of the American Dream* (NY: Public Affairs, 2012)

BARESEL, James, **"How "Democracy" Lost Its Meaning**, *Chronicles*, March 2025

BEDOYA, Alvaro B., **"How I Became A Populist,"** *The New Republic*, November 2025

BELZER, David and David Wayne, *Corporate Conspiracies: How Wall Street Took Over Washington* (NY: Skyhorse Publishing, 2017)

BENEN, Steve, *The Imposters: How the Republicans Quit Governing and Seized American Politics* (NY: HarperCollins Publishers, 2020)

BOSSCHE, van den, **"The Message for Today" in Orwell's '1984,"** *The New York Times*, January 1, 1984

BRILL, Steve, *Tailspin: The People and Forces behind America's Fifty-Year Fall – and Those Fighting to Reverse It* (NY: Alfred A. Knoph, 2018)

BURLEIGH, Nina, *"The Making of Dark Money King,"* *The New Republic*, June 2023

CAPPINS, McKay, *"Newt Gingrich Says You're Welcome,"* *Atlantic* (November 2018)

CHAYES, Sarah, *On Corruption in America: And What Is at Stake* (NY: Alfred A. Knoph,2020)

COHEN, Adam, *Supreme Inequality: The Supreme Court's Fifty-Year Battle for a More Unjust America* (NY: Penguin Books, 2020)

COHEN, Brian Tyler, *Shameless: Republicans' Deliberate Dysfunction and the Battle to Preserve Democracy* (NY: HarperCollins, 2024)

CRIER, Catherine, *Patriot Acts: What Americans Must Do To Save the Republic* (NY: Threshold Editions, 2011)

COCKBURN, Andrew, *The Spoils of War:Power, Profit and the American War Machine* (NY: Verso Books, 2021)

COX, Ana Marie, *"How the Radical Right Captured the Culture,"* *The New Republic*, May 2025

CHURCHILL, Ward, *A Little Matter of Genocide: Holocaust and Denial in the Americas 1492 to the Present* (SF: City Lights Books, 1997)

COVERT, Bryce, **"Everyone Must Go: Hedge-Fund Owners Drive Sears and Toys "R" Us into Bankruptcy and Put Thousands of People Out of Work,"** *The Nation, May 6, 2019*

CULP, Doug, **"Option for the Poor and Vulnerable," Parable**, *November/ December 2025*

DERBER, Charles and Yale *MAGRASS, The Surplus American: How the 1% Is Making Us Redundant* (Boulder, CO: Paradigm Publishers, 2012)

ERLSTEIN, Rick, *Reaganland: America's Right Turn 1976-1980* (NY: Simon & Schuster, 2020)

ELDERMAN, Peter, *Not A Crime Be Poor: The Criminalization of Poverty in America* (NY: The New Press, 2017)

ELLIS, Joseph J., *American Dialogue: The Founders And Us* (NY: Alfred A. Knoph, 2018)

ENRICH, David, *Murder the Truth: Fear, the First Amendment, and A Secret Campaign to Protect the Powerful* (Ann Arbor, MI: University of Michigan Press, 2025)

FORNIER, Joseph R. I, ed., *The Language of Liberty: The Political Speeches and Writings of Abraham Lincoln* (Washington, D.C.: Regnery Publishing, Inc., 2009)

FRANKS, Thomas, *The Wrecking Crew: How Conservatives Ruined Government, Enriched Themselves, and Beggared the Nation* (NY: Holt Paperbacks, 2008)

GATES, Henry Louis, *Stony the Road: Reconstruction, White Supremacy, and the Rise of Jim Crow* (NY: Penguin Press, 2019)

CANNON, Bruce, *A Generation of Sociopaths: How the Baby Boomer Betrayed America* (NY: Hachette Books, 2017)

GIGANTES, Philippe, *Power and Greed: A Short History of the World* (NY: Carrol & Graf Publishers, 2002)

GLAUDE, Eddie S., Jr., *Democracy in Black: How Race Still Enslaves the American Soul* (NY: Crown Publishers, 2016)

GREIDER, William M., *Who Will Tell the People: The Betrayal ofAmerican Democracy* (NY: Simon and Schuster, 1992)

GRUNDY, George W., *Death of a Nation: 9/11 and the Rise of Fascism in America* (NY: Skyhorse Publishing, 2017)

GUENDELSBERGER, Emily, *On the Clock: What Low-Wage Work Did to Me and How It Drives America Insane* (NY: Little, Brown and Company, 2019)

HARTMANN, Thom, *Screwed: The Undeclared War Against the Middle Class* (San Francisco, CA 2006)

HARTMANN, Thom, *The Crash of 2016: The Plot to Destroy America* (NY: Twelve, 2014)

HARTMANN, Thom, *The Hidden History of Monopolies: How Big Business Destroyed the American Dream* (Oakland, CA: Berrett-Koehler Publishers, Inc, 2020)

HARTMANN, Thom, *The Hidden History of American Oligarchy: Reclaiming Our Democracy from the Ruling Class* (Oakland, CA: Berrett-Koehler Publishers, Inc, 2021)

HARTMANN, Thom, *The Hidden History of the American Dream: Demise of the Middle Class – and How to Rescue Our Future* (NY: Penguin Random House, 2024)

HARTMANN, Thom: *The Last President: A Broken Man, A Corrupt Party, and A World on the Brink* (NY: Penguin Random House, 2025)

HEDGES, Chris, *American Fascists: The Christian Right and the War on America* (NY: Free Press, 2006)
HEDGES, Chris, T*he World As It Is: Dispatches on the Myth of Human Progress* (NY: Nation Books, 2013)

HIGHTOWER, Jim, *Thieves in High Places: They've Stolen Our Country - And It's Time To Take It Back* (NY: Viking Penguin, 2003)

HONEY, Michael K., *To the Promised Land: Martin Luther* Company, 2018)

HOBSON, John, *Imperialism: A Study* (London, 2011)

HUDSON, Michael, *Super Capitalism: The Economic Strategy of American Empire* (Islet Publishing, 2021)

JONES, Matt with Chris TOMLIN, *Mitch Please!: How Mitch McConnell Sold Out Kentucky (and America, Too)*, (NY: Simon & Schuster, 2020)

KENDZIOR, Sarah, *Hiding in Plain Sight: The Invention of Donald Trump and the Erosion of America* (NY: Flatiron Book, 2020)

KARL, Jonathon, *Betrayal: The Final Act of the Trump Show* (NY: Penguin Random House, 2022)

KLEINKNECHT, William, *The Man Who Sold the World: Ronald Reagan and the Betrayal of Main Street America* (NY: Nation Books, 2009)

KOVALIK, Dan, *The Plot to Control the World: How the US Spent Billions to Change the Outcome of Elections Around the World* (NY: Skyhorse Publishing, 2018)

LEFEBVRE, Georges, *The Coming of the French Revolution* (Princeton University Press, 1973)

LEHMANN, Chris, **"Lobbying for War,"** The Nation, November 27-December 4, 2023

LINDSEY, Lawrence B., *Conspiracies of the Ruling Class: How to Break Their Grip Forever* (NY: Simon & Schuster, 2016)

LITMAN, Leath, *Lawless: How the Supreme Court Runs On Conservatives Grievance, Fringe Theories, and Bad Vibes* (Atria/One Signal Publishers, 2025)

LOFGREN, Mike, *The Deep State: The Fall of the Constitution and the Rise of a Shadow Government* (NY: Viking Penguin, 2016)

LOFGREN, Mike, *The Party Is Over: How Republicans Went Crazy, Democrats Became Useless, and the Middle Class Got Shafted* (NY: Viking Penguin, 2012)

MACLEAN, Nancy, *Democracy in Chains: The Deep History of the Radical Right's Plan for America* (NY: Viking, 2017)

MARSHALL, Jonathan, *Dark Quadrant: Organized Crime, Big Business, and the Corruption of American Democracy From Truman to Trump* (NY: Rowan & Littlefield, 2021)

MAYER, Jane, *Dark Money: The Hidden History of the Billionaires Behind the Rise of the Radical Right* (NY: Doubleday, 2016)

McCULLOUGH, David, *The American Spirit: Who We Are and What We Stand for* (NY: Simon & Schuster, 2017)

McGARITY, Thomas, *Freedom to Harm: The Lasting Legacy of the Laissez Faire Revival* (New Haven, Yale University Press, 2013)

MEACHAM, Jon, *The Soul of America: The Battle for Our Better Angels* (NY: Penguin Random House, 2018)

MILBANK, Dana, *The Destructionists: The Twenty-Five Year Crack-Up of the Republican Party* (NY: Doubleday, 2022)

NATIONS, Scott, *A History of the United States in Five Crashes Stock Market Meltdowns That Defined A Nation* (NY: HarperCollins, 2017)

OLLER, John, *White Shoe: How a New Breed of Wall Street Lawyers Changed Big Business and the American Century* (NY: Penguin Random House, 2019),

PERLSTEIN, Rick, **"Prophets of Instability: How Finance Broke the Modern Corporations,"** The Nation, March 30, 2020

PIERUCCI, Frederic with Matthew *Aron, The American Trap, My Battle to Expose America's Secret Economic War Against the Rest of the World* (NY: Hodder & Stoughton, 2019)
PILLING, David, *The Growth Delusion: Wealth, Poverty, and the Well-Being of Nations* (Tim Duggan Books, 2018)

PILLING, David, *The Delusion of Growth: Wealth, Poverty, and the Well-Being of Nations* (NY: Tim Duggan Books, 2018)

POWELL, Lewis F., Jr., *Memorandum: "Attack on the American Free Enterprise System," August 23, 1971* (Chamber of Commerce, Washington, D.C.)

QUART, Alissa, *Squeezed: Why American Families Can't Afford America* (NY: HarperCollins, 2018)

RAMUS, Jack, *The Scourge of Neoliberalism: US Economic Policy from Reagan to Trump* (Atlanta, GA, Clarity Press, Inc., 2020)

RAMUS, Jack, *The War At Home: The Corporate Offensive from Ronald Reagan to George W. Bush* (San Ramon, CA: Kyklos Publicans, 2006)

REICH, Robert B., *Supercapitalism: The Transformation of Business, Democracy, and Everyday Life* (NY: Alfred Knopf, 2007)

REICH, Robert B., *Beyond Outrage: What Has Gone Wrong with Our Economy and Our Democracy, and How to Fix It* (NY: Vintage Books, 2012)

REICH, Robert B., *Saving Capitalism: For the Many, Not the Few* (NY: Alfred A. Knoph, 2015)

REICH, Robert B, *The Common Good* (Alfred A. Knopf, 2018)

REID-HENRY, Simon, *Empire of Democracy: The Remaking of the West Since the Cold War, 1971-2017* (NY: Simon & Schuster, 2019)

RICHARDSON, Heather Cox, **"The Fight for Our America,"** *The New Republic*, November 2023

RESSA, Maria, *How to Stand Up to a Dictator: The Fight for Our Future* (NY: HarperCollins, 2023)

ROBERTSON, Phil, *The Theft of America's Soul: Blowing the Lid Off the Lies That Are Destroying Our Country* (Nashville, TN: Nelson Books, 2011)

RUSSELL, Dick, *Horsemen of the Apocalypse: The Men Who Are Destroying Life on Earth and What It Means for Our Children* (NY: Skyhorse Publishing, 2017)

SARGENT, Greg, **"Trump's Sloe-Burn Authoritarianism,"** *The New Republic*, October 2024

SCHIFF, Adam, *Midnight in Washington: How We Almost Lost Our Democracy and Still Could* (NY: Random House, 2021)

SEIB, Gerald F., *We Should Have Seen It Coming: From Reagan to Trump – A Front-Row Seat to a Political Revolution* (NY: Random House, 2020)

SMITH, Hedrick, *Who Stole the American Dream* (NY: Random House, 2012)

SHAXSON, Rick, **"Rural America Doesn't Have to Starve,"** The Nation, March 30, 2020

SNYDER, Timothy, *On Freedom* (NY: Vintage Publishing, 2004)

SNYDER, Timothy, *On Tyranny* (NY: Tim Duggan Books, 2017)

STANLEY, Jason, *How Fascism Works: The Politics of US and Them,* (NY: Random House, 2018)

STERNBERG, Joseph C., *The Theft of a Decade: How the Baby Boomers Stole the Millennials' Econonic Future* (NY: PublicAffairs, 2019)

STEVENS, Stuart, *How the Republican Party Became Donald Trump* (NY: Alfred A. Knopf, 2020)

STEVENS, Stuart, *The Conspiracy to End America: Five Ways My Old Party Is Driving Ou Democracy to Autocracy* (Alfred A. Knopf, 2023)

STIGLITZ, Joseph E., *People, Power, and Profits: Progressive Capitalism for an Age of Discontent* (NY: W. Norton & Company, 2019)

STOLLER, Matt, *Goliath: The 100-Year War between Monopoly Power and Democracy* (NY: Simon & Schuster, 2019)

STONE, Oliver and Peter **KUZNICK,** *The Untold History of the United States* (Gallery Books, 2019)

SULLIVAN, Teresa A., Elizabeth **WARREN**, and Jay Lawrence **WESTBROOK,** *The Fragile Middle Class: Americans in Debt* (New Haven: Yale University Press, 2020)

TOMASKY, Michael, ed., *What American Fascism Would Look Like: A Special Report,* *The New Republic,* June 2024

TOMASKY, Michael, ed., **How Democracy Dies**, *The New Republic*, January/February 2025

TOMASKY, Michael, ed., The Obscene Wealth Issue, *The New Republic*, July-August 2025

SUNSTEIN, Cass R., *Can It Happen Here? Authoritarianism in America* (NY: HarperCollins Publishers, 2018)

TAYLOR, Miles, Blowback: *A Warning to Save Democracy from the Next Trump* (NY: Atria Books, 2023)

TIRADO, Linda, *Hand to Mouth: Living In Bootstrap America* (NY: Berkley Books, 2014)

TOMASKY, Michael, **"Donald Trump Against America,"** *The New Republic*, June 2023

TOMASKY, Michael, ed., *What American Fascism Would Look Like: A Special Report,* *The New Republic,* June 2024

TOMASKY, Michael, ed., *The Obscene Wealth Issue, The New Republic*, July-August 2025

WALLACE, Vice President *Henry, Remarks on Fascism in America, The New York Times*, April 9, 1944

WHITEHOUSE, Sheldon & Melanie Wachtell **STINNETT**, *Captured: The Corporate Infiltration of American Democracy* (NY: The New Press, 2017)

WINANT, Gabriel, **"No Going Back: The Power and Limits of the Anti-Monopolist Traditions,"** The Nation, February 3, 2020

WOLFF, Richard D., *Democracy at Work: A Cure for Capitalis*m (Chicago, IL: Haymarket Books, 2012)

WOLFF, Richard D, *The Sickness is the System: When Capitalism Fails to Save Us from the Pandemic or Itself* (NY: Democracy at Work, 2020)

WOLIN, Sheldon S, *Democracy Incorporated: Managed Democracy and the Specter of Inverted Totalitarianism* (Princeton, NJ: Princeton University Press, 2008)

ZELIZER, Julian E, *Burning Down the House: Newt Gingrich and the Rise of The New Republican Party* (NY: Penguin Book, 2020)

ZINN, Howard, *A People's History of the United States, 1492-2001* (NY: Harper Company, 1980/1999)

FOR
DEMOCRACY
TO
LET FREEDOM RING
EVERY VOTE MATTERS

POEM

TO BEGIN ANEW

I SEE the
Torch of Liberty
Beckoning a proud
Democratic people to a
NEW AGE OF FREEDOM

I HEAR the sound
Of distant drums
Echoing Freedom's
Call To LIBERTY AND
JUSTICE FOR ALL

I HEAR
The toll of
LIBERTY'S BELL
Ringing for a great
PATRIOTIC RENEWAL

I HEAR above
The din of battle
The Soul of America

174

Cry out to the
American Spirit ...

FEAR NOT AMERICA,
THE LIGHT OF A NEW DAWN
BECKONS TO
BRIGHTEN YOUR TOMORROW

PROJECT 2025

The People's Guide to Project 2025
democracyforward.org/join-2025

PROJECT 2025 IS AMONG THE THE MOST PROFOUND THREATS TO THE AMERICAN PEOPLE

We read Project 2025's entire 900+ page "Mandate for Leadership" so that you don't have to. What we discovered Project 2025 is a systemic, ruthless plan to undermine the quality of life of millions of Americans, remove critical protections and dismantle programs for communities across the nation, and prioritize special interests and ideological extremism over people.

From attacking overtime pay, student loans, and reproductive rights, to allowing more discrimination, pollution, and price gouging, those behind Project 2025 are preparing to go to incredible lengths to create a country only for some, not for all of us.

If these plans are enacted, which Project 2025's authors claim can happen without congressional approval, 4.3 million people could lose overtime protections, 40 million people could have their food assistance reduced, 220,000 American jobs could be lost, and much, much, more. The stakes are higher than ever for democracy and for people.

These threats aren't hypothetical. These are their real plans.

The Heritage Foundation and the 100+ organizations that make up the Project 2025 Advisory Board have mapped out exactly how they will achieve their extreme ends. They aim to try and carry out many of the most troubling proposals through an anti-democratic president and political loyalists installed in the executive branch, without waiting for congressional action. And, while many of these plans are unlawful, winning in court is not guaranteed given that the same far-right movement that is behind Project 2025 has shaped our current court system.

To combat the threats posed by Project 2025, we have to first understand them.

What follows are some of the most dangerous proposals that make up Project 2025, specifically those that they plan to implement through federal agencies and a far-right executive branch.

The majority of Americans share the same values and priorities, but Project 2025 wants to push an extreme, out-of-touch agenda on all of us. **By reading this guide and sharing it, we can begin to address these threats and go on offense towards building a bold, inclusive democracy for all people.**

PROJECT 2025

The Project 2025 Presidential Transition Project is a well-funded (eight-figure) effort of the Heritage Foundation and more than 100 organizations to enable a future anti-democratic presidential administration to take swift, far-right action that would cut wages for working people, dismantle social safety net programs, reverse decades of progress for civil rights, redefine the way our society operates, and undermine our economy.

A central pillar of Project 2025 is the "Mandate for Leadership," a 900+ page policy playbook authored by former Trump administration officials and other extremists that provides a radical vision for our nation and a roadmap to implement it.

PROJECT 2025 SNAPSHOT

Proposals from Project 2025, discussed in detail throughout this guide, that they claim could be implemented through executive branch action alone — so without new legislation — include:

- Cut overtime protections for 4.3 million worker;

- Stop efforts to lower prescription drug prices;

- Limit access to food assistance, which an average of more than 40 million people in 21.6 million households rely on monthly;

- Eliminate the Head Start early education program, which serves over 1 million children annually;

- Cut American Rescue Plan (ARP) programs that have created or saved 220,000 jobs

- Restrict access to medication abortion;

- Push more of the 33 million people enrolled in Medicare towards Medicare Advantage and other worse, private options

- Expose the 368,000 children in foster care to risk of increased discrimination;

- Deny students in 25 states and Washington, D.C. access to student loans because their state provides in-state tuition to undocumented immigrants;

- Roll back civil rights protections across multiple fronts, including cutting diversity, equity, and inclusion-related (DEI) programs and LGBTQ+ rights in health care, education, and workplaces.

EXPLORE PROJECT 2025

Cut Wages, Create Unsafe Workplaces, and Destabilize Our Economy

Project 2025 would enable corporations to cut overtime pay, relax worker safety rules, allow workplace discrimination, and more.

Make It Harder for Americans to Make Ends Meet

A strong democracy is one where people have the resources they need to thrive, not worry about how they will make ends meet. Project 2025 proposals would only make daily life harder for people – with fewer people able to access food assistance and affordable early education, less support for veterans with disabilities, and cuts to support for farmers.

Restrict Reproductive Rights and Access to Health Care

Despite the majority of Americans supporting comprehensive health care and reproductive freedom, Project 2025 would prefer a far different reality. Their attacks would undermine Medicare, keep prescription drug prices high, and restrict access to reproductive care.

Enable Discrimination Across Society

Threatened by decades of progress in advancing civil rights and equality for all, the authors of Project 2025 want to create a country that allows for more discrimination where we live, study, work, and play — and roll back hard-fought victories by our movements for progress.

Set Polluters Loose and Undo Climate Action

We've waited decades for meaningful and robust federal action to combat climate change and protect people from the harms of pollution. Project 2025 couldn't care less about these threats — and now they want to destroy our hard-fought gains.

Make Education Unaffordable and Unwelcoming

Our public schools are foundational to our democracy. When special interests undermine public schools, they undermine the ability of students from all backgrounds to learn, feel safe in their community, and develop skills and knowledge that enable students to thrive. If Project 2025 has their way, our public schools could be stripped of funding, protections for students, and high-quality curricula.

Undermine Government's Ability to Deliver for People

Civil servants are federal employees who work and live in all 50 states — the more than 2 million people who keep our air clean, water safe, consumers protected, and mail delivered. Attacks on the nation's civil service are attacks on the government's ability to work for the people.

Undermine Business Growth and Innovation

By risking the health of American businesses and our workforce, Project 2025 threatens all of us who rely on a thriving, robust economy.

Target Immigrants and Expand Executive Power

Project 2025 would cut off asylum at the border, slash access to legal immigration pathways, use local resources to carry out mass deportations and mass detention, and hurt immigrant kids and families.

Project 2025 is Already Underway in the Courts

If a far-right president was empowered to politicize the Department of Justice (DOJ), it could refuse to defend the freedoms, protections, and programs under attack in key cases, ensuring that these aspects of Project 2025 are enshrined into law. Far-right extremists are already working to impose some of the most unpopular proposals in Project 2025 in states across the country. Even as some try to distance themselves from Project 2025's proposals or to question its practicability in light of current backlash, it is clear that the movement is deeply tied to the core tenets of the project.

THE THREATS FROM PROJECT 2025

This *People's Guide* only begins to catalog the people and communities who would be harmed if a future presidential administration began to implement Project 2025's proposals. Businesses and industry across the country could be harmed not just from the lack of data collection discussed above, but also from proposals to politicize the Federal Reserve or to restrict free trade. Our country's national security itself, too, is threatened by proposals to concentrate military decision making, further undermine our intelligence agencies, or promote isolationist policies. We continue to analyze these policies and their harms to people, and expect to release updated versions of the People's Guide with reports on the threats that would make it harder to run a business, put our security at risk, and more.

POEM

FREEDOM RISING

THOUGH I WALK
The
Empty darkness
Of misery and despair
Forsaken and forgotten

THOUGH I LONG
For
An America of
FREEDOM,
EQUALITY & JUSTICE

I AM
A CITIZEN
OF
DEMOCRACY

CONFIDENT
The SPIRIT OF AMERICA
Will rise out of the darkness
TRIUMPHANT for an
America of LIBERTY
AND JUSTICE
FOR ALL

"Freedom of speech is a principle pillar of a free government; when this support is taken away, the constitution of a free society is dissolved, and tyranny is erected on its ruins."
Benjamin Franklin

"To protest against injustice is the foundation of all our American democracy."
Thurgood Marshall